PIANO
Adventures® *by Nancy and Randall Faber*
THE BASIC PIANO METHOD

_____ is sightreading this book!
(your name)

Production Coordinator: Jon Ophoff
Cover: Terpstra Design, San Francisco
Illustrations: Erika LeBarre

ISBN 978-1-61677-639-8
Copyright © 2013 Dovetree Productions, Inc.
c/o FABER PIANO ADVENTURES, 3042 Creek Dr., Ann Arbor, MI 48108.

CHART YOUR PROGRESS

Sightreading for Lesson Book p. 6
Moon Walker............................ 6-9

DAY 1   DAY 2   DAY 3   DAY 4   DAY 5

Sightreading for Lesson Book p. 8
Almost Like a Dream 10-13

DAY 1   DAY 2   DAY 3   DAY 4   DAY 5

Sightreading for Lesson Book p. 9
Sounds from the Gumdrop Factory 14-17

DAY 1   DAY 2   DAY 3   DAY 4   DAY 5

Sightreading for Lesson Book pp. 12-13
Spanish Caballero 18-23

DAY 1   DAY 2   DAY 3   DAY 4   DAY 5

Sightreading for Lesson Book p. 15
Boxcar Rumble............................ 24-27

DAY 1   DAY 2   DAY 3   DAY 4   DAY 5

Sightreading for Lesson Book pp. 18-19
Shave and a Haircut 28-31

DAY 1   DAY 2   DAY 3   DAY 4   DAY 5

Sightreading for Lesson Book pp. 22-23
Jumpin' Jazz Cat.......................... 32-35

DAY 1   DAY 2   DAY 3   DAY 4   DAY 5

Sightreading for Lesson Book pp. 24-25
Down by the Bay.......................... 36-39

DAY 1   DAY 2   DAY 3   DAY 4   DAY 5

Sightreading for Lesson Book pp. 26-27
The Ice Skaters 40-45

DAY 1   DAY 2   DAY 3   DAY 4   DAY 5

Sightreading for Lesson Book pp. 30-31
Vive la France! 46-49

DAY 1   DAY 2   DAY 3   DAY 4   DAY 5

Sightreading for Lesson Book pp. 34-35
Horse-Drawn Carriage 50-55

DAY 1   DAY 2   DAY 3   DAY 4   DAY 5

Sightreading for Lesson Book pp. 38-39
Beach Party................................ 56-59

DAY 1   DAY 2   DAY 3   DAY 4   DAY 5

SIGHTREADING

SIGHTREADING SKILL

Good sightreading skill is a powerful asset for the developing musician. It makes every step of music-making easier. With the right tools and a little work, sightreading skill can be developed to great benefit.

In language literacy, the reader must not only identify single words, but also group words together for understanding. Similarly, music reading involves more than note naming. The sightreader tracks horizontally and vertically, observing intervals and contour while gleaning familiar patterns that make up the musical context.

As students read beyond a five-finger pattern, coach with the following:

1. Notice the two signatures: key signature and time signature

2. Take a moment to scan the music with sharp eyes for

   rhythm patterns

   melodic patterns

   hand shifts

   dynamics

3. Find the *hardest-looking* measure. Count and play it in your mind.

4. Set a slow tempo with one free "count-off" measure.

The decoding skill of sightreading requires repetition within familiar musical contexts. In other words, pattern recognition develops by seeing a lot of the same patterns. This book offers carefully composed variations to sharpen perception of the new against a backdrop of the familiar. Consistent with the literacy analogy, the musician must not simply identify single notes, but also group notes into meaningful musical patterns.

How to Use

This book is organized into sets of 5 exercises, for 5 days of practice. Each set provides variations on a piece from the **2nd Edition Piano Adventures® Level 2B Lesson Book.** Play one exercise a day, completing one set per week.

Though the student is not required to repeatedly "practice" the sightreading exercise, each should be repeated as indicated by the repeat sign. For an extra workout, play each of the previous exercises in the set before playing the new exercise of the day.

Curiosity and Fun

The "Don't Practice This!" motto is a bold statement which has an obvious psychological impact. It reminds us that sightreading is indeed "the first time through" and it reminds us to keep the activity fun.

The comic-style "educational art" draws students through each set of pages by building curiosity. Characters such as marching gumdrops and a Spanish caballero encourage the elementary reader with musical questions and creative exercises. Each sightreading page presents a new "learning vignette" in a spirit of fun.

Level of Difficulty

Some language experts say that a student should not stumble on more than three or four words per page when reading at the appropriate level of difficulty. Similarly, a sightreader should not stumble on more than three or four notes per page of music. This Sightreading Book is carefully written to match the Level 2B Lesson Book and to provide well-graded sightreading material.

Marking Progress

Students are encouraged to draw a large **X** over each completed exercise. This instruction is so out of the ordinary that students find it immensely satisfying to mark their progress in this way.

Some students may exclaim about the thickness of the book! They soon are rewarded to find how fast they can move through it. Indeed, with confidence increasing, the student can take pride in moving to completion of this very large book…and do so with a crescendo of achievement.

Instructions to Student

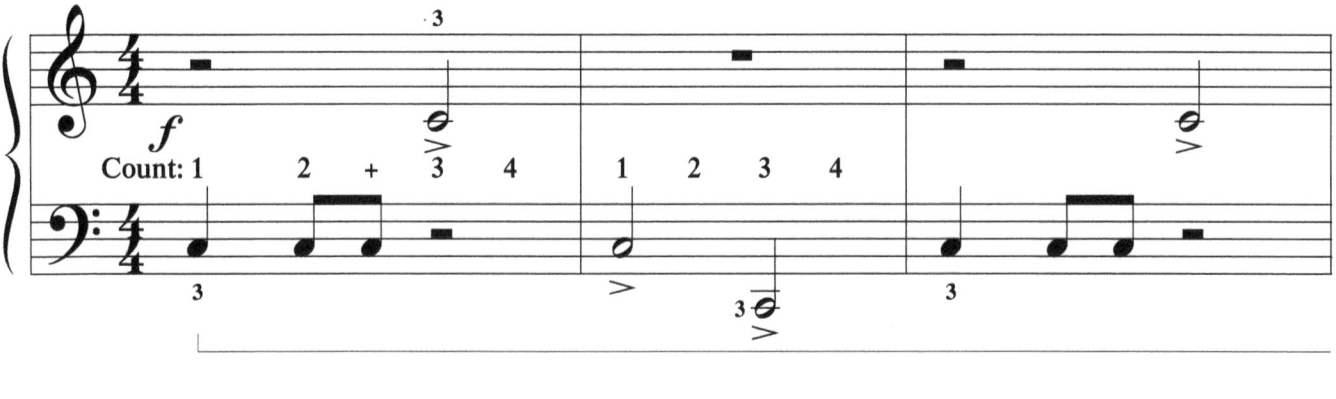

DAY 1: Moon Walker

Watch for the octave shifts from C to C.
Use only finger 3's for this set of pieces.

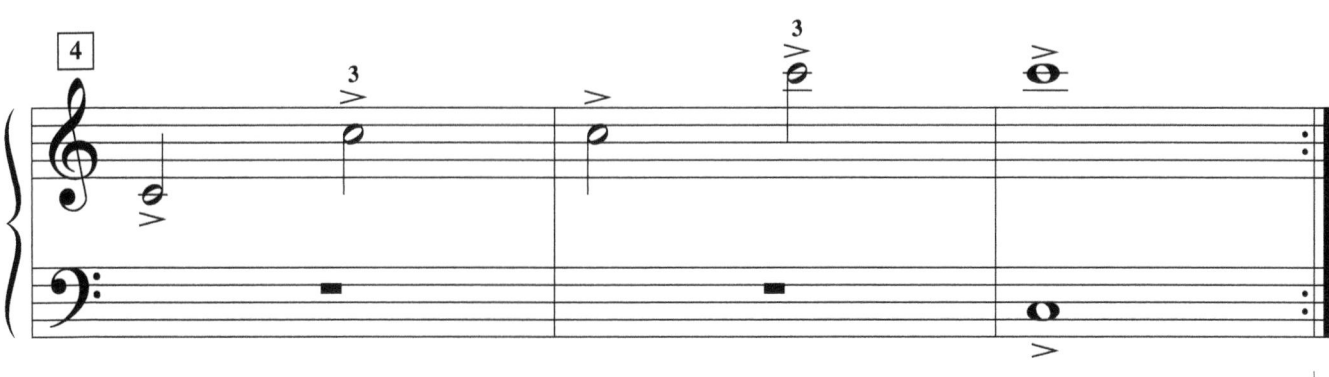

DAY 2: Moon Walker

Scan the music. Notice the R.H. octave shifts.

DAY 3: Moon Walker

Notice the *piano* and *forte* signs.

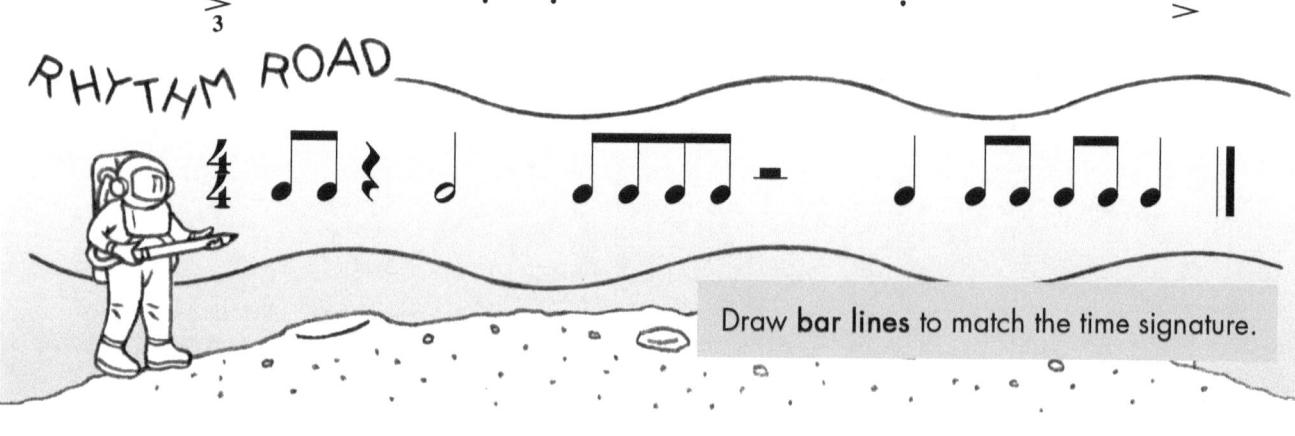

Draw **bar lines** to match the time signature.

DAY 4: Moon Walker

DON'T
PRACTICE
THIS!

Scan the music. Notice the octave shifts for each hand.

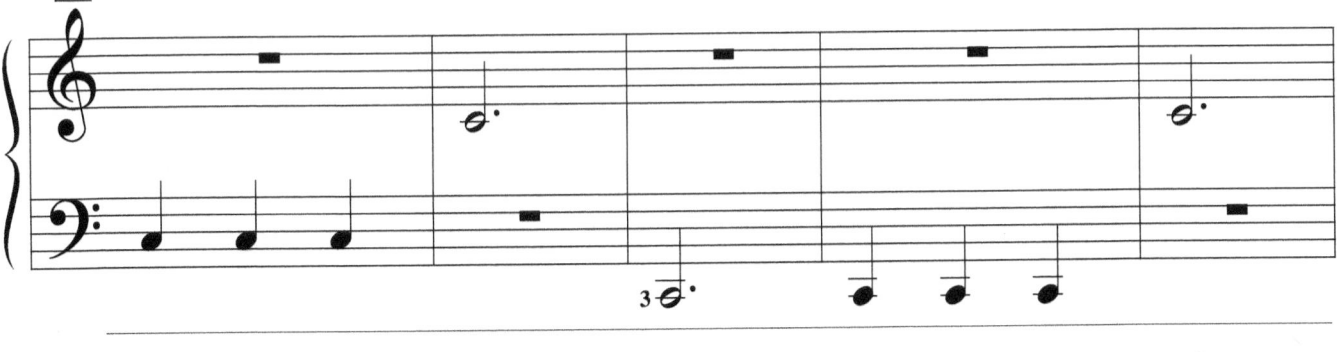

Draw an X through the two **incorrect measures**.

8

RHYTHM ROAD

4/4

Write **two measures** of your own 4/4 rhythm! Then tap for your teacher.

DAY 5 CONGRATS!

DAY 5: Moon Walker

DON'T PRACTICE THIS!

Scan the music. What two letter names are used?

f

Count: 1 2 3 4   1 2 3 4   1 2 3 4   1 2 3 4

(prepare L.H.)

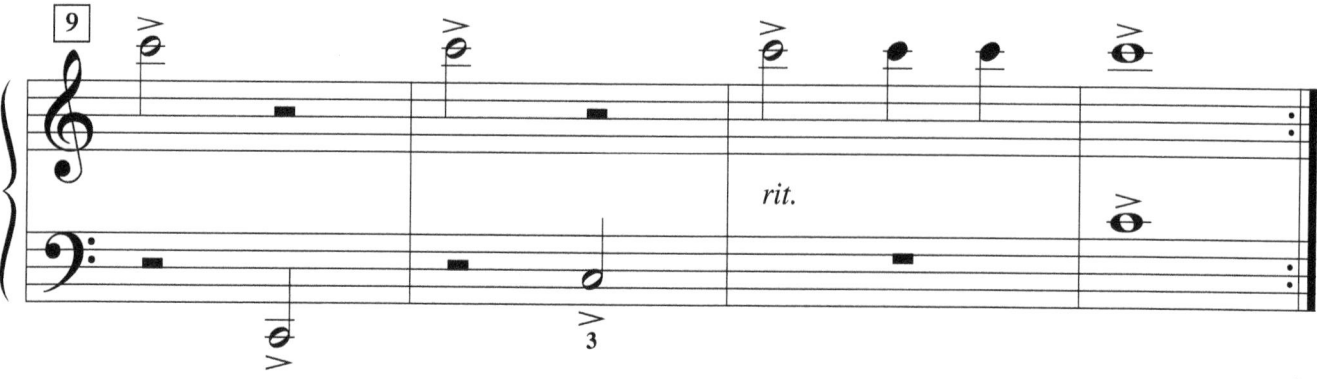

rit.

Can you find the **quarter rest** in the design?

DAY 1: Almost Like a Dream

_____ **Major/minor 5-Finger Scale (circle one)**

DON'T
PRACTICE
THIS!

DAY 2: Almost Like a Dream

_____ **Major/minor 5-Finger Scale**

Plan the L.H. position changes before you play.

Count: 1   +   2   +   3   +   4   +

DAY 3: Almost Like a Dream

DON'T PRACTICE THIS!

Write 1 + 2 + 3 + 4 + under the correct notes.

DAY 4: Almost Like a Dream

Plan the L.H. position changes before you play.

Count: 1 2 3 4 1 + 2 + 3 4

Connect the rhythms with **equal beats.**

RHYTHM ROAD

CONGRATS

$\frac{4}{4}$

Write **two measures** of your own 4/4 rhythm. Use **8th notes** in each measure.

DAY 5: Almost Like a Dream

DON'T PRACTICE THIS!

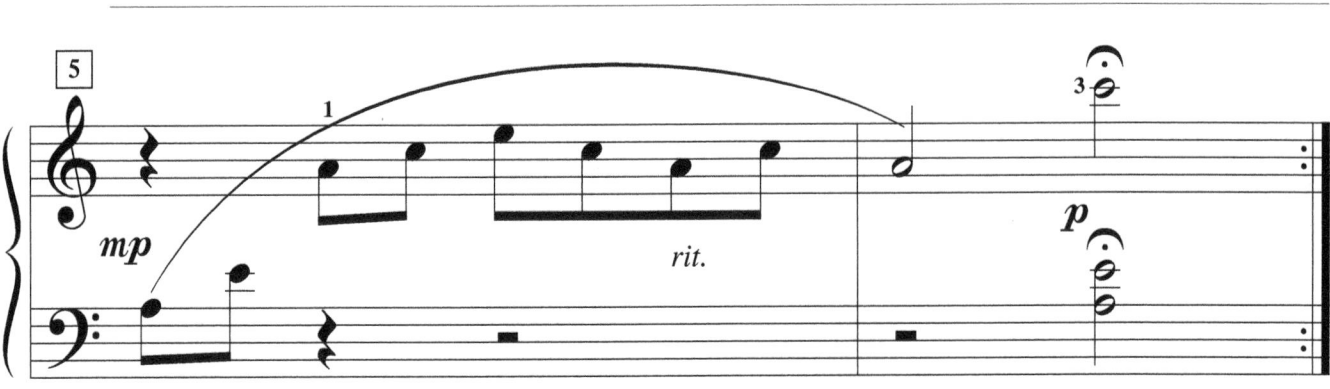

DAY 1: Sounds from the Gumdrop Factory

_____ Major/minor 5-Finger Scale (circle one)

DON'T PRACTICE THIS!

DAY 2: Sounds from the Gumdrop Factory

_____ Major/minor 5-Finger Scale

DON'T PRACTICE THIS!

Draw **bar lines** to match the time signature.

DAY 3: Sounds from the Gumdrop Factory

Plan the R.H. chord changes before you play.

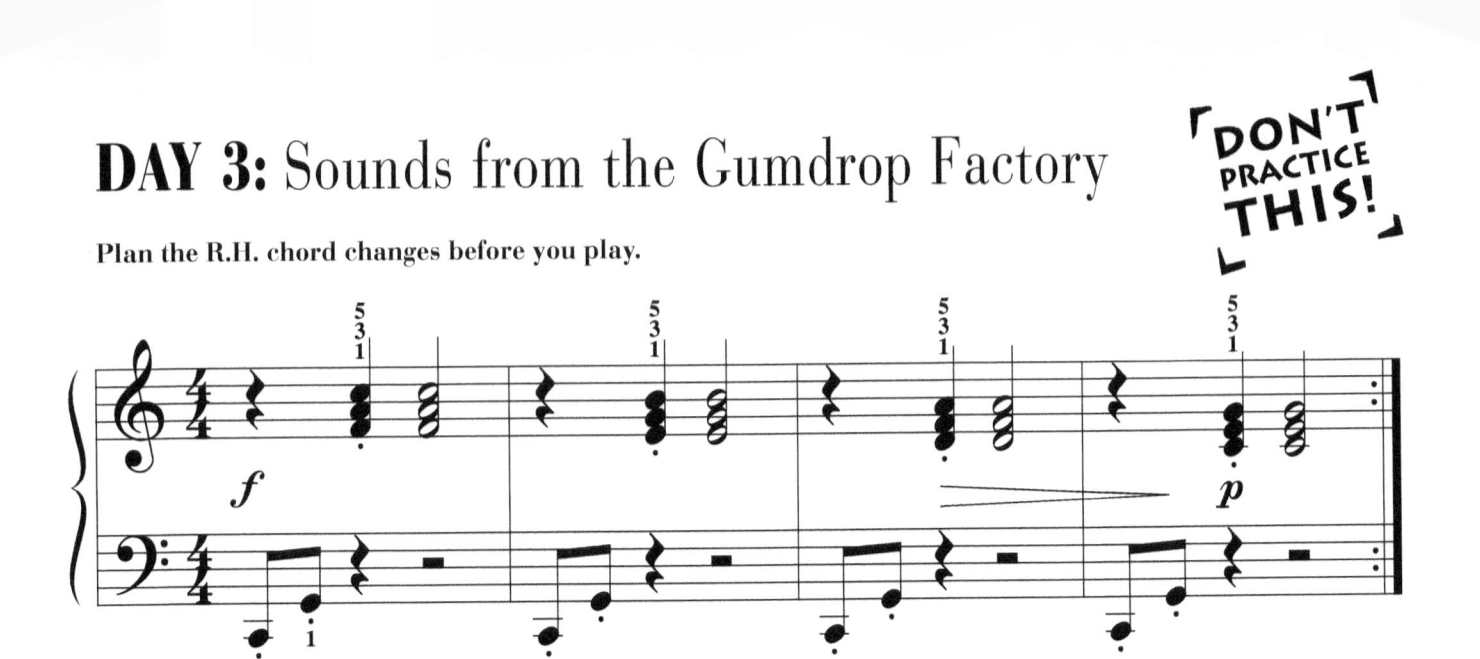

DAY 4: Sounds from the Gumdrop Factory

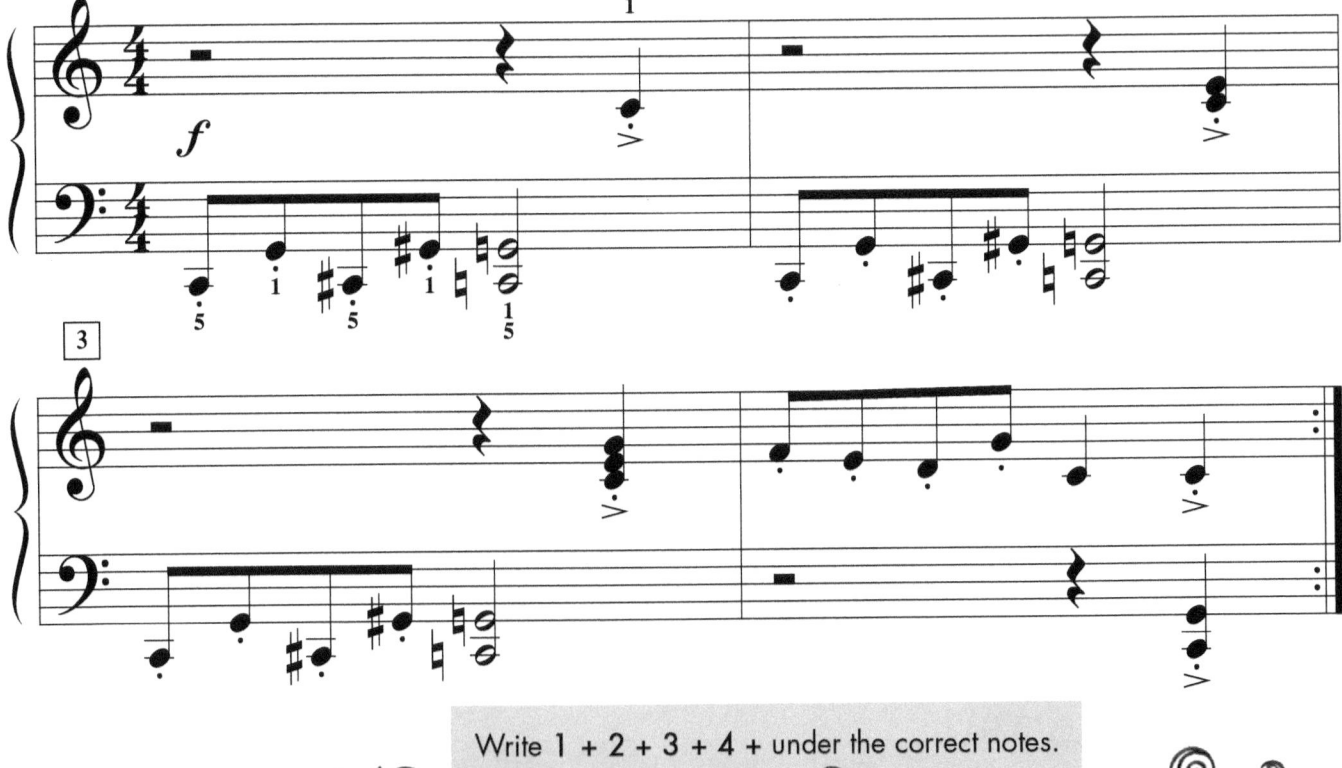

Write 1 + 2 + 3 + 4 + under the correct notes.

RHYTHM ROAD

16

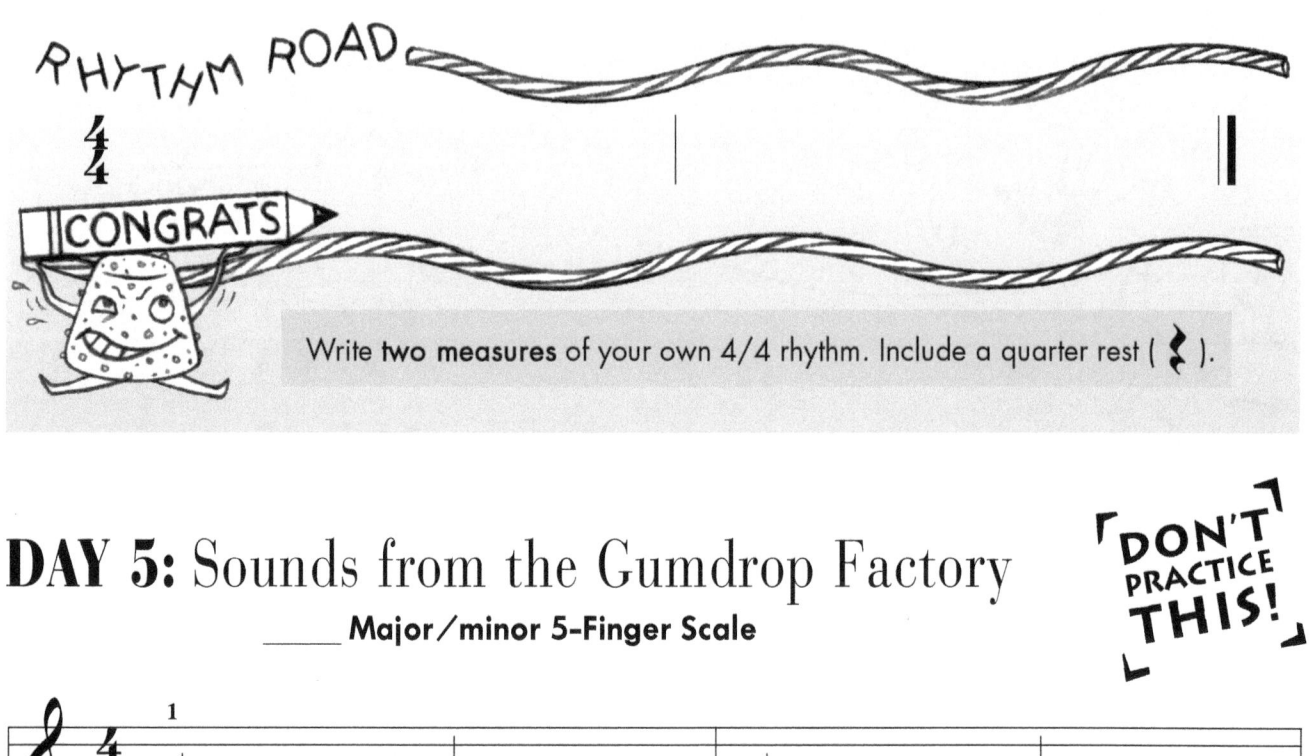

Write **two measures** of your own 4/4 rhythm. Include a quarter rest (𝄽).

DAY 5: Sounds from the Gumdrop Factory

_____ **Major/minor 5-Finger Scale**

DON'T PRACTICE **THIS!**

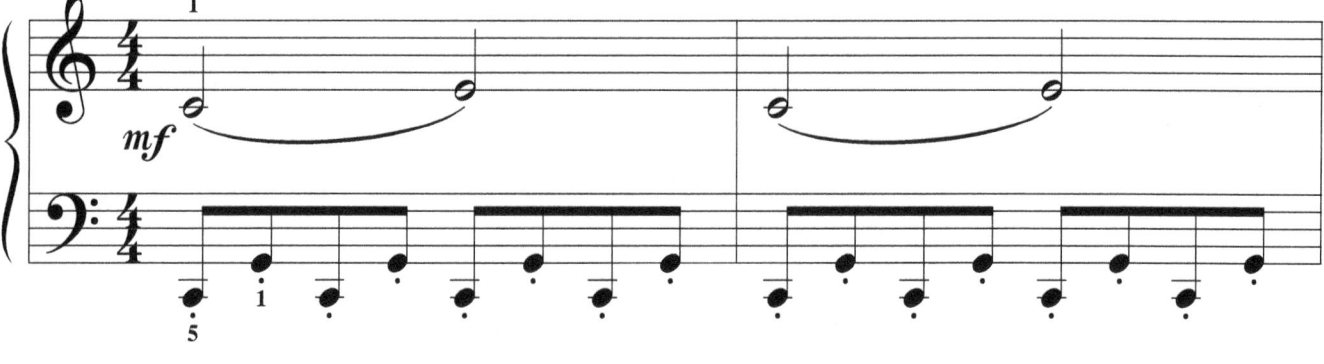

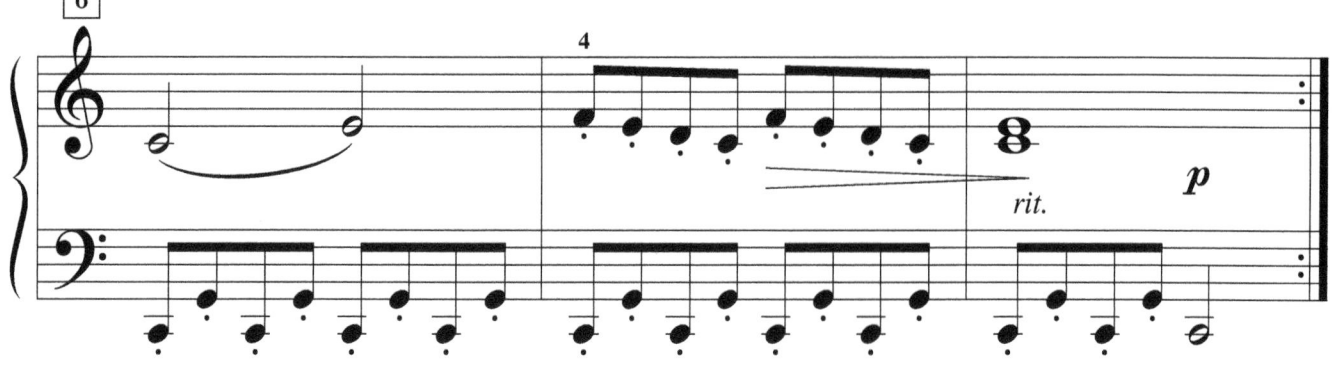

DAY 1: Spanish Caballero

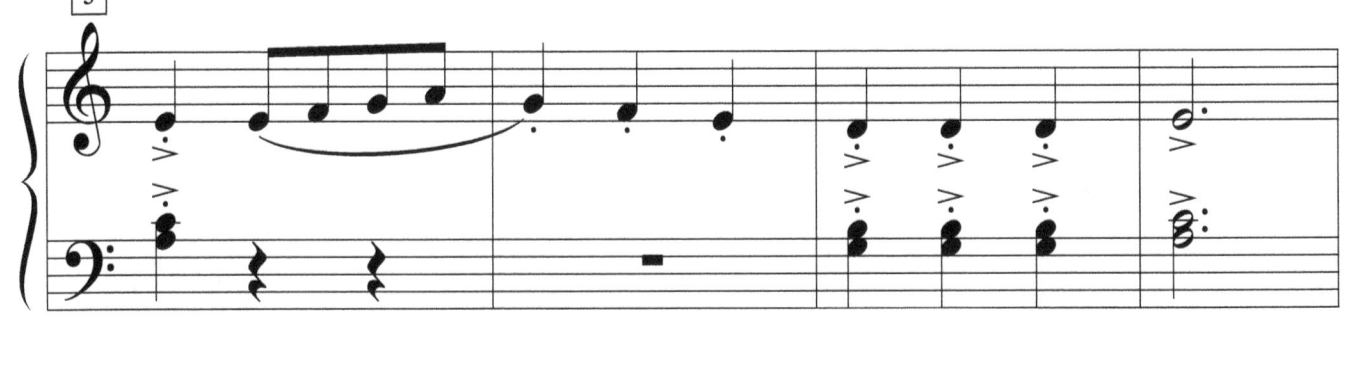

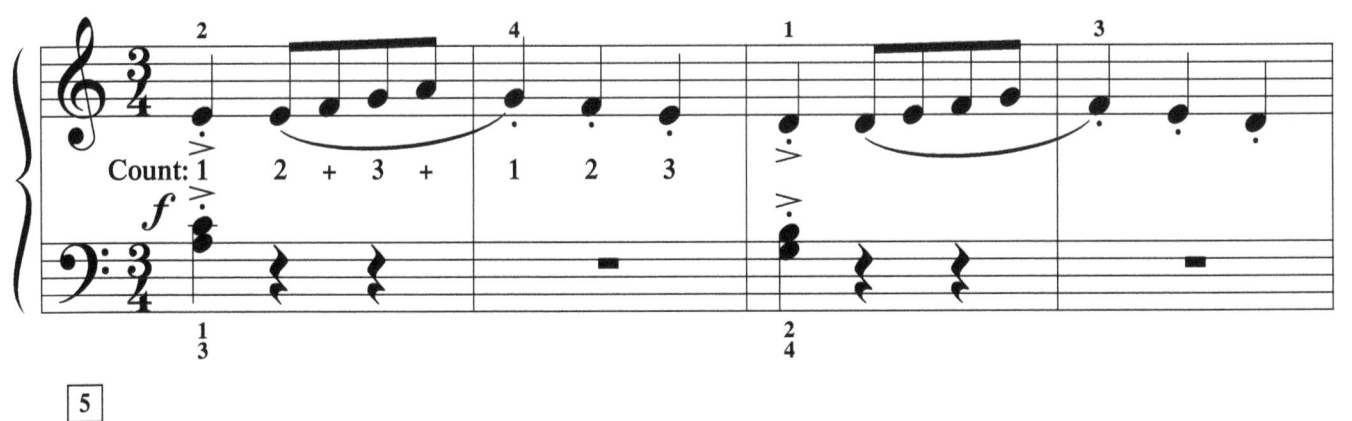

DAY 3: Spanish Caballero

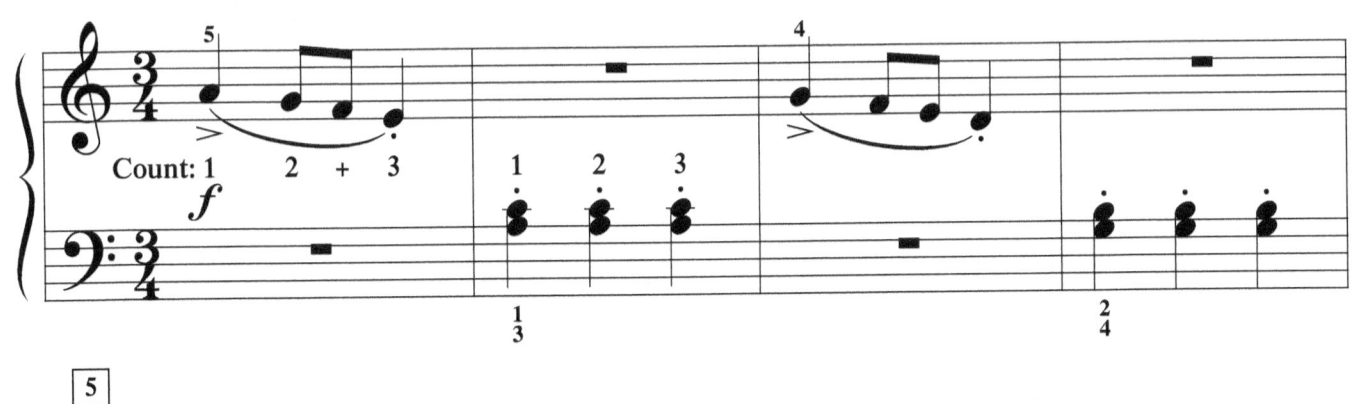

Draw **bar lines** to match the time signature.
Hint: How many beats does a whole rest receive in 3/4 time?

RHYTHM ROAD

DAY 4: Spanish Caballero

DON'T PRACTICE THIS!

What interval does the R.H. play?

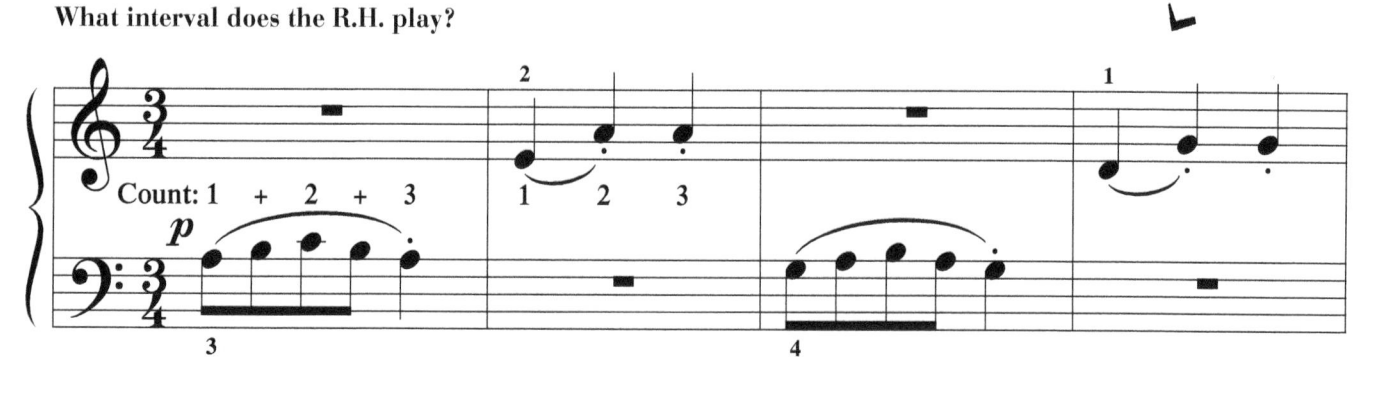

DAY 5: Spanish Caballero

Hint: Scan the music carefully before playing.
Notice the chord pattern moves down in measures 1-8.

Fill in the **empty measures** on both pages with your own 3/4 rhythms.

Notice both hands return to the opening position.

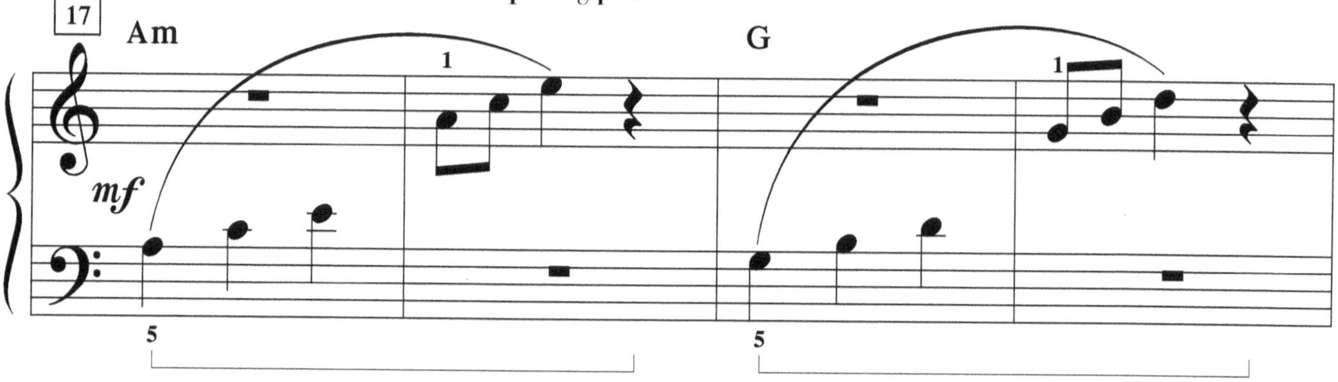

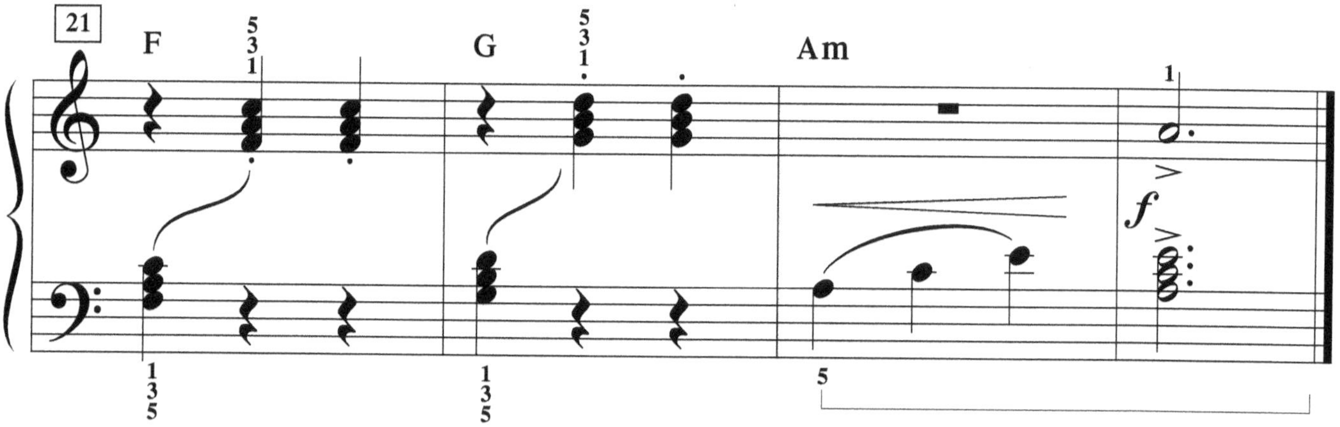

DAY 1: Boxcar Rumble

Scan the music. Notice the changes for the two L.H. intervals.

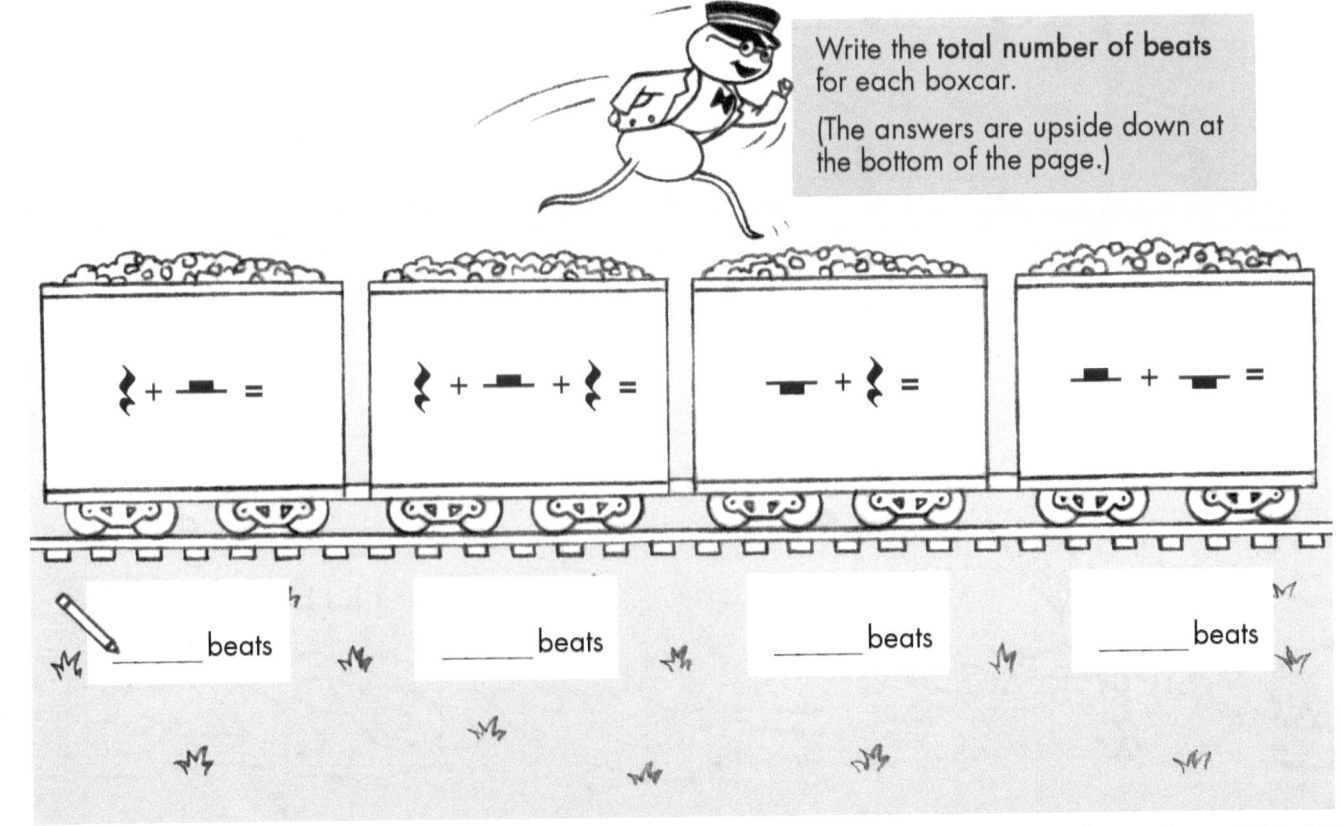

Write the **total number of beats** for each boxcar.

(The answers are upside down at the bottom of the page.)

_____ beats   _____ beats   _____ beats   _____ beats

Answers: 3 beats, 4 beats, 5 beats, 6 beats

Write 1 2 3 4 under the correct beats.

DAY 2: Boxcar Rumble

Scan and notice the R.H. changes.
Scan again and notice the L.H. changes.

DON'T
PRACTICE
THIS!

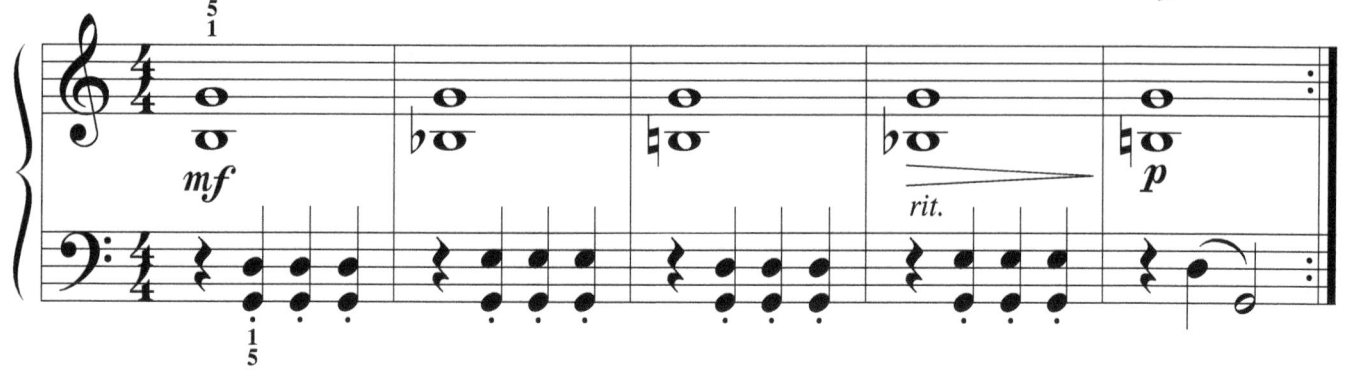

DAY 3: Boxcar Rumble

Finger measures 1 and 2 silently on the keys before playing.

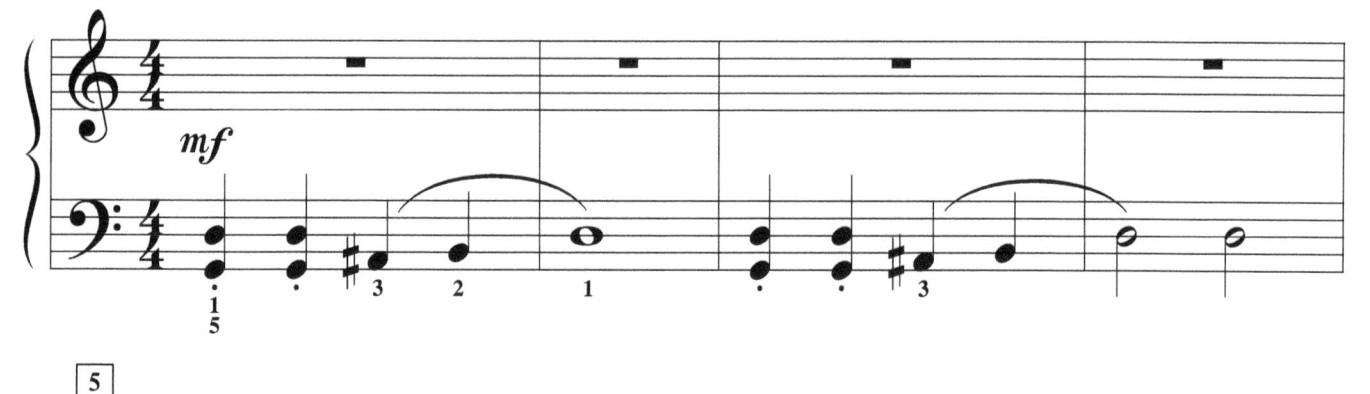

25

DAY 4: Boxcar Rumble

DON'T PRACTICE THIS!

Scan the music. Notice the L.H. intervals change quickly.
Hint: Prepare your right foot on the damper pedal before starting.

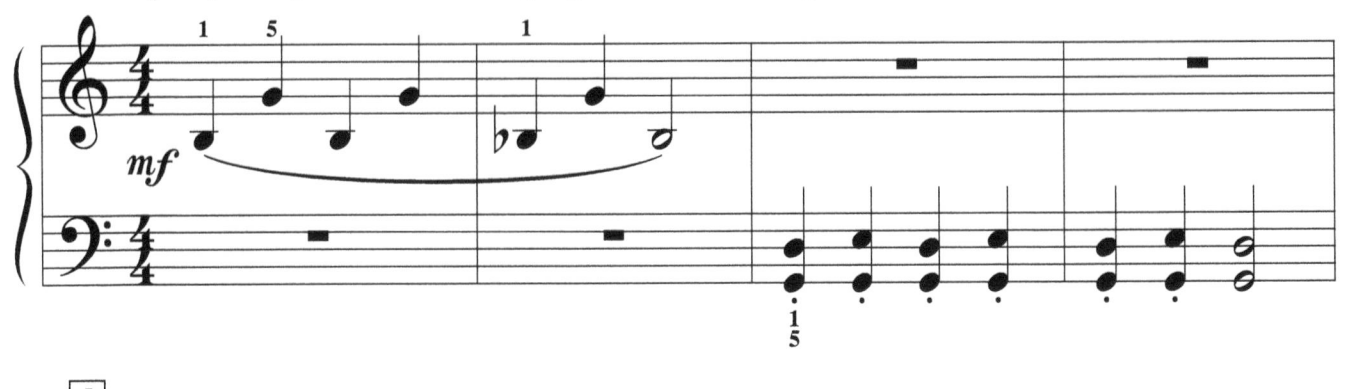

Put an X through the two **incorrect measures**.

Write **three measures** of your own 4/4 rhythm. Use several **rests**.

DAY 5: Boxcar Rumble

Notice the descending R.H. sixths.

DON'T PRACTICE THIS!

DAY 1: Shave and a Haircut

Hint: Count-off, "1 + 2 + 3 +" and begin the pick-up notes on "4 +".

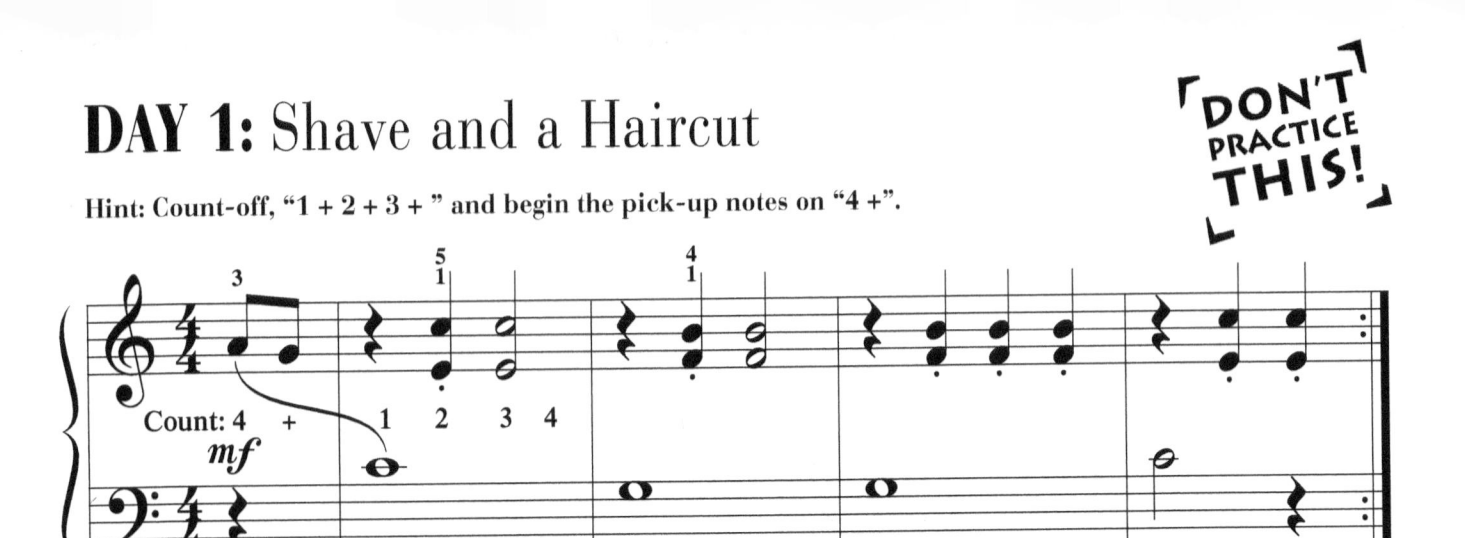

DAY 2: Shave and a Haircut

Hint: Prepare your L.H. before starting.

On what beat does this rhythm begin?

1 2 3 4 (circle)

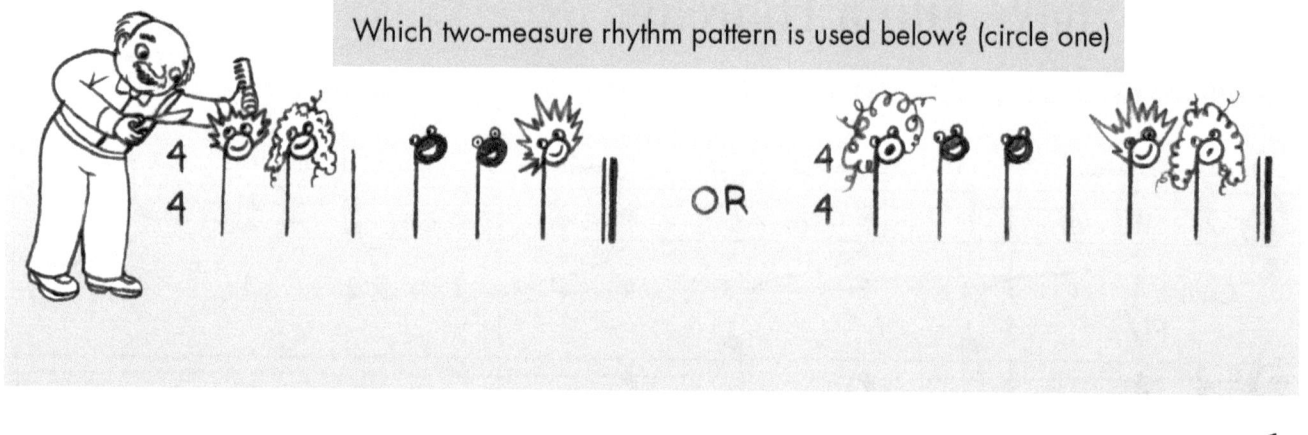

Which two-measure rhythm pattern is used below? (circle one)

DAY 3: Shave and a Haircut

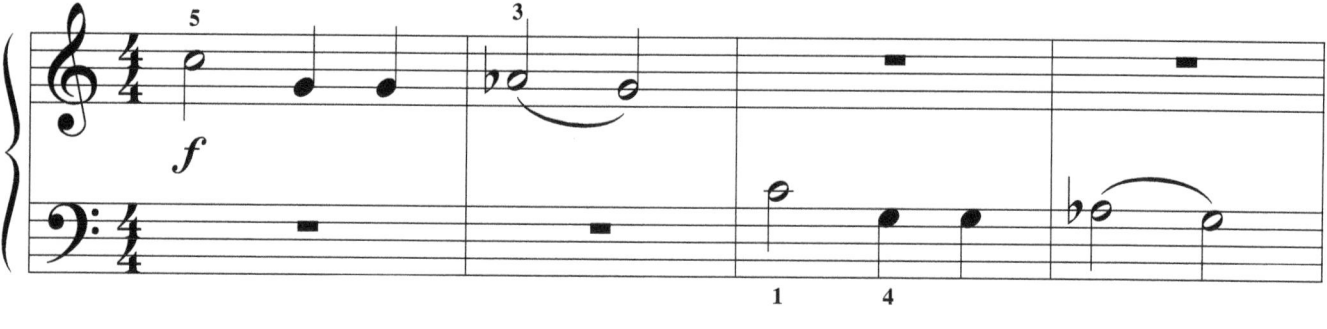

DON'T PRACTICE THIS!

DAY 4: Shave and a Haircut

How will you count off? Hint: See DAY 1.

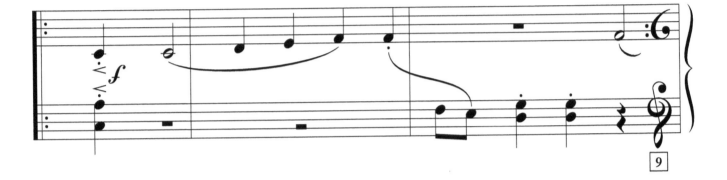

Draw bar lines for this rhythm. Draw a double bar line at the end.

How many measures use only **half steps**? (circle)

DAY 5: Shave and a Haircut

Scan the music. Notice the R.H. position changes.
Hint: Prepare your L.H. before starting.

DON'T
PRACTICE
THIS!

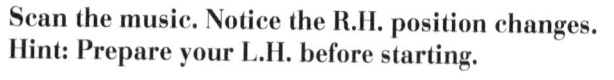

DAY 1: Jumpin' Jazz Cat

Key of _____ Major

DAY 2: Jumpin' Jazz Cat

Key of _____ Major

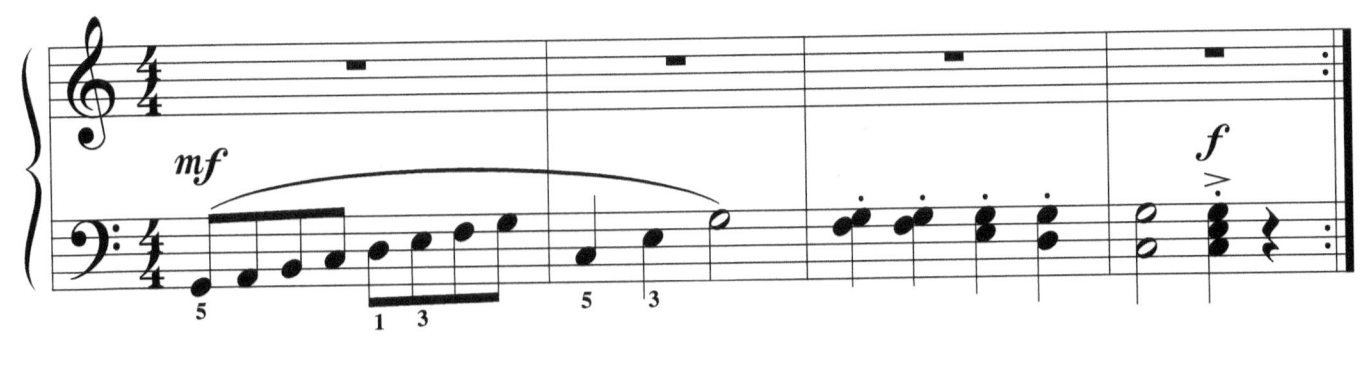

Circle the jazz cat playing the whole note **leading tone**.

DAY 3: Jumpin' Jazz Cat

Key of _____ Major

DON'T PRACTICE THIS!

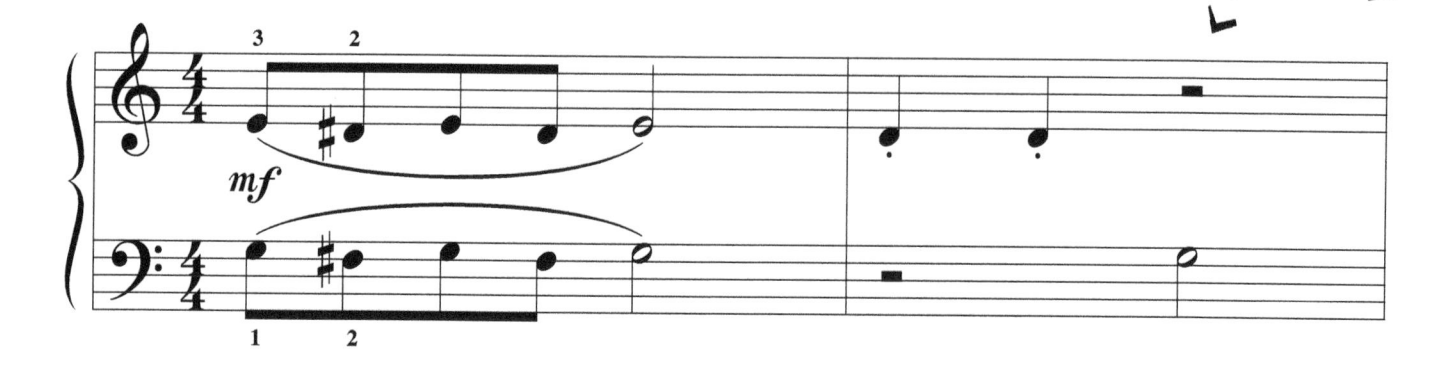

Circle the measure with the **correct counting**.

DAY 4: Jumpin' Jazz Cat

Key of _____ Major

DON'T PRACTICE THIS!

Notice the L.H. shift at measure 3. Name the bass note and find its location on the keyboard.

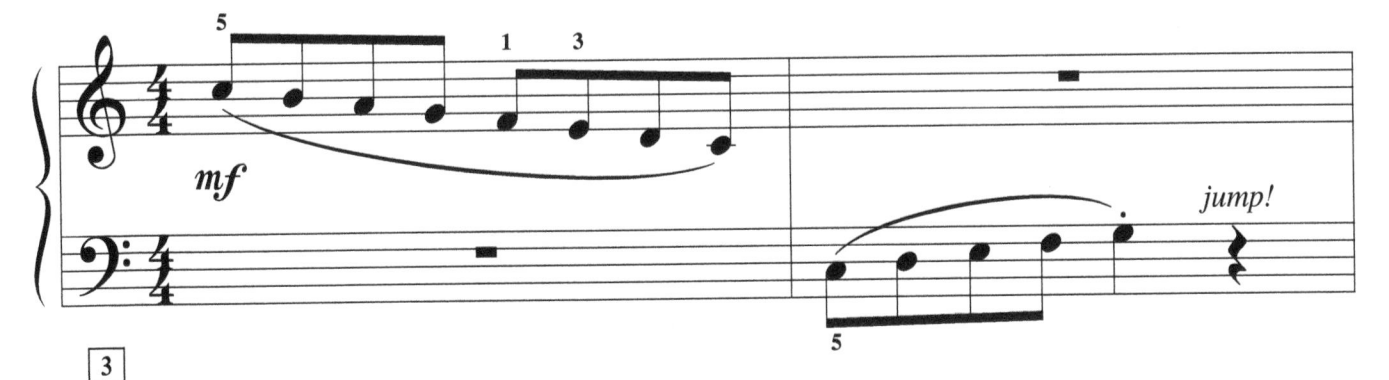

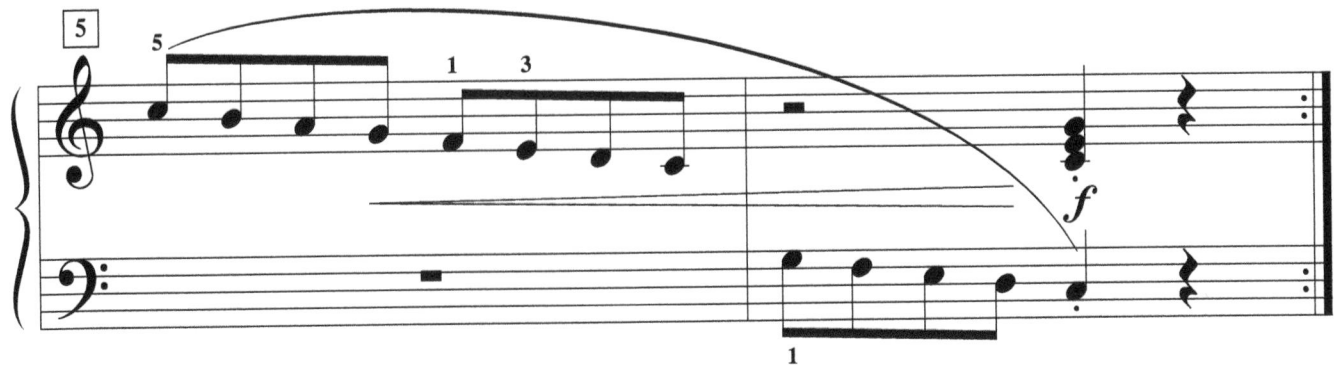

DAY 5: Jumpin' Jazz Cat

Key of _____ Major

Notice the starting note for each L.H. scale.
Will you need to shift?

Write **two measures** of your own 4/4 rhythm for the jazz cats to play.

(you write)   (you write)

35

Does the crescendo start on the **I** or **V7 chord**? (circle one)

Did you ever see a chord, surfing on a board?

DAY 1: Down by the Bay

Key of _____ Major

DON'T PRACTICE THIS!

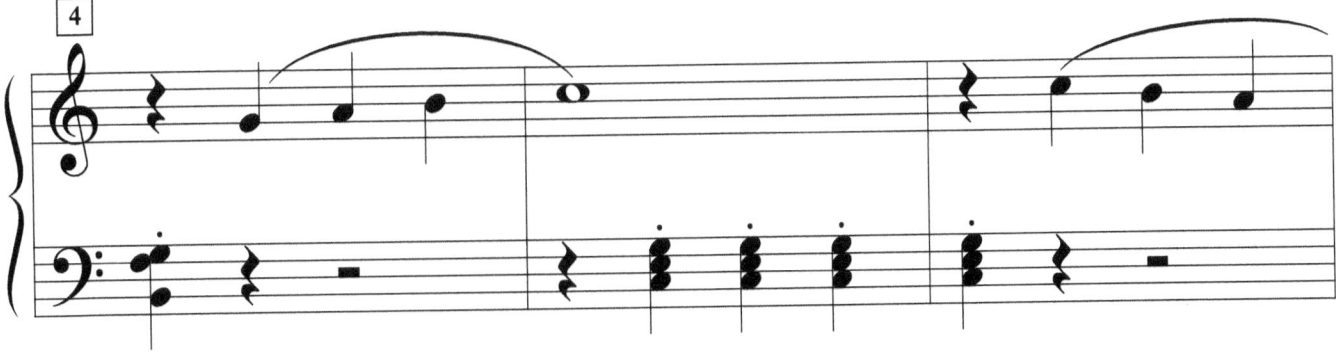

DAY 2: Down by the Bay

Key of _____ Major

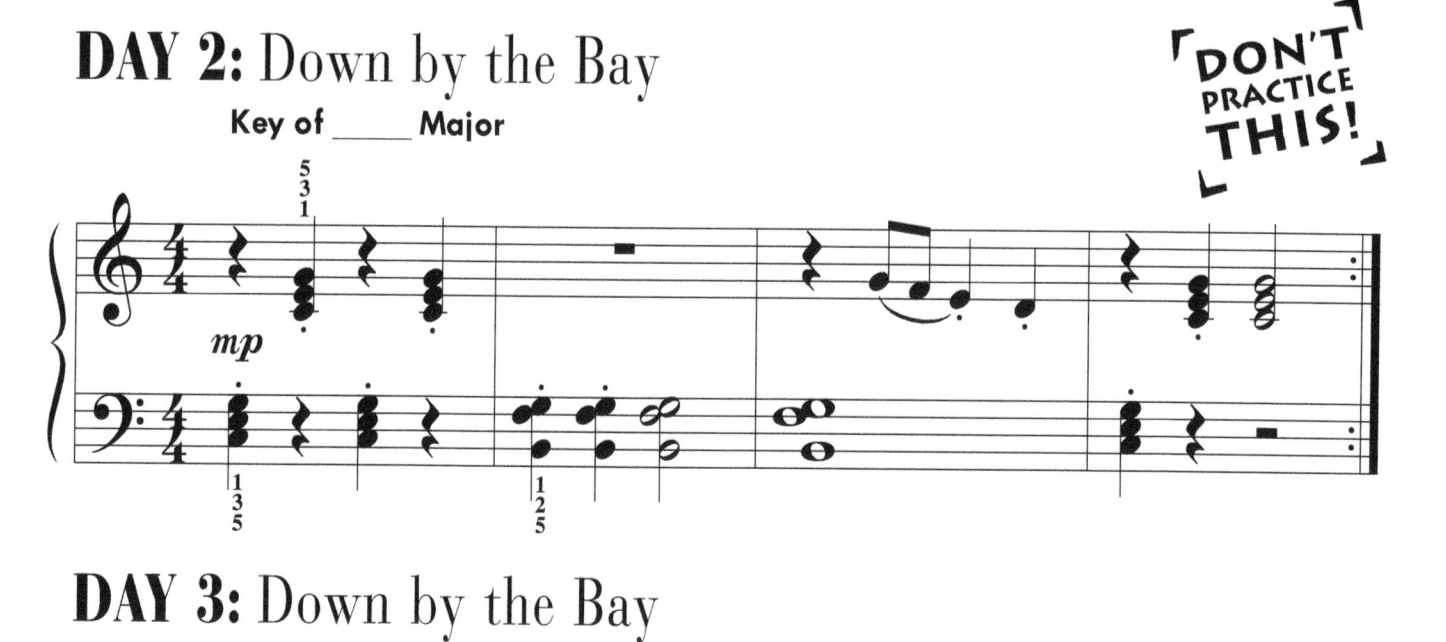

DON'T PRACTICE THIS!

DAY 3: Down by the Bay

Key of _____ Major

Hint: Count-off, "1-2-3-4, 1" and begin the pick-up notes.

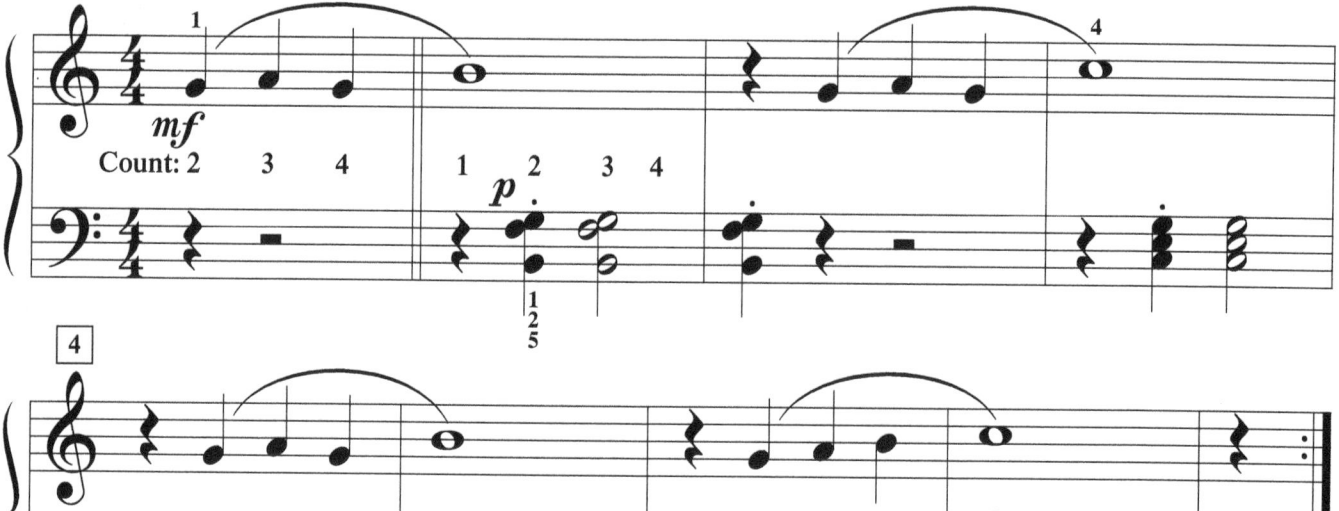

Did you ever see a note, rowing in a boat?

Which day begins with the **V7 chord**? (circle a fish)

DAY 4: Down by the Bay

Key of _____ Major

DON'T PRACTICE THIS!

Hint: Count-off, "1-2-3-4, 1-2" and begin the pick-up notes.

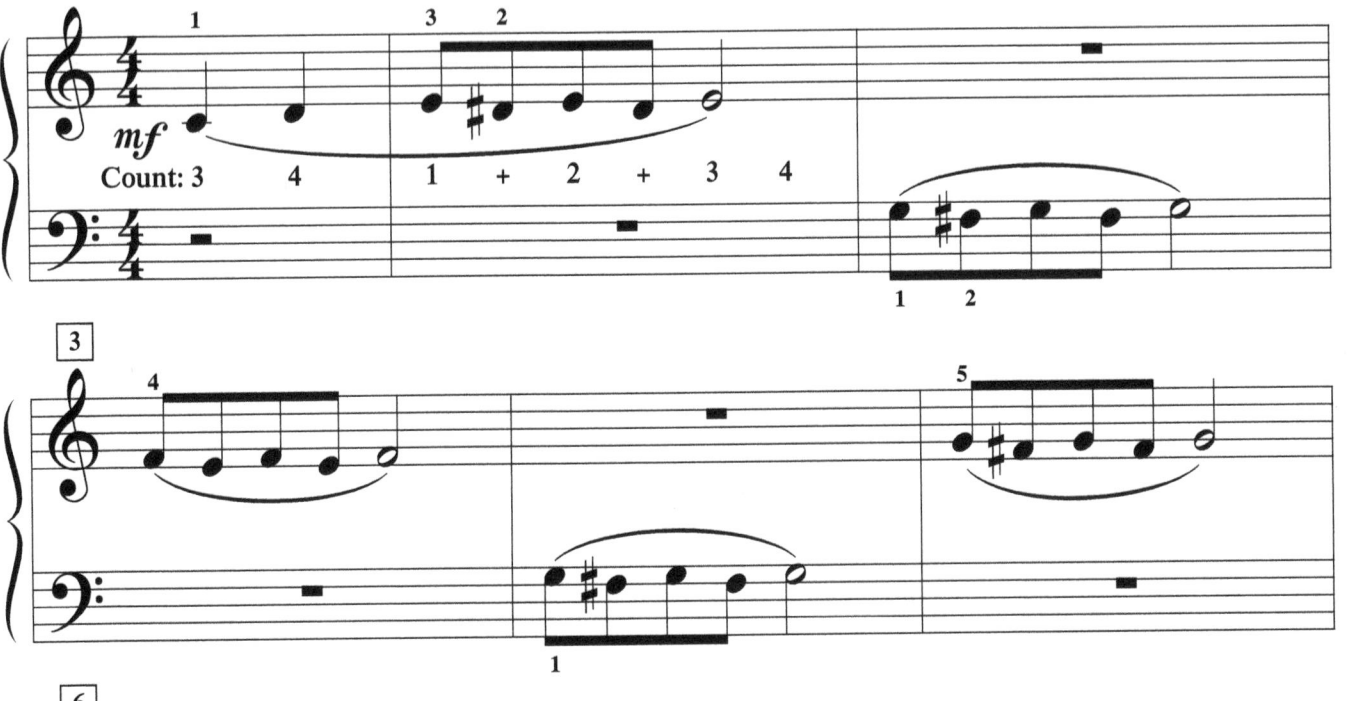

Have you ever seen a staff, learning how to laugh?

HA! HA!

38

DAY 5: Down by the Bay

Key of _____ Major

DON'T PRACTICE THIS!

DAY 1: The Ice Skaters

Key of _____ Major

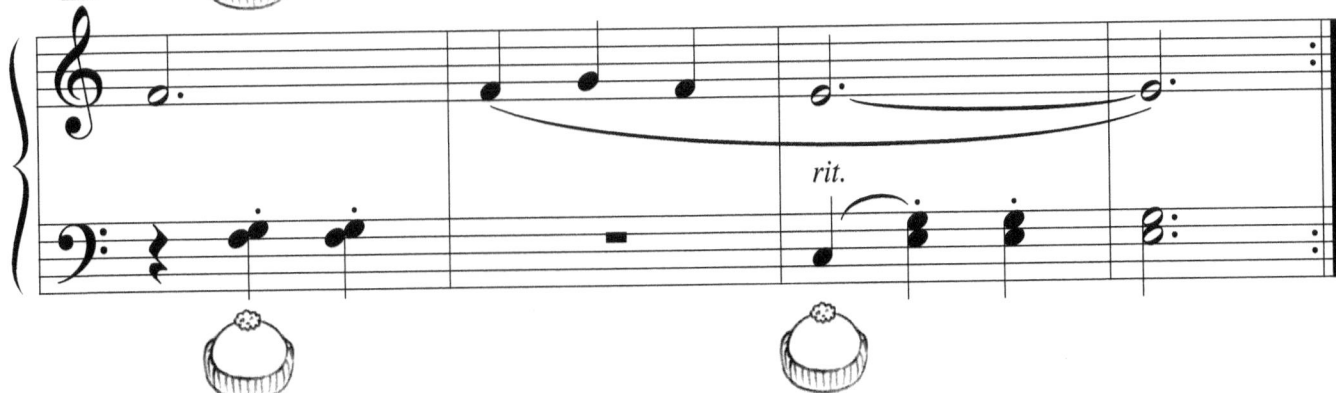

40

DAY 2: The Ice Skaters

Key of _____ Major

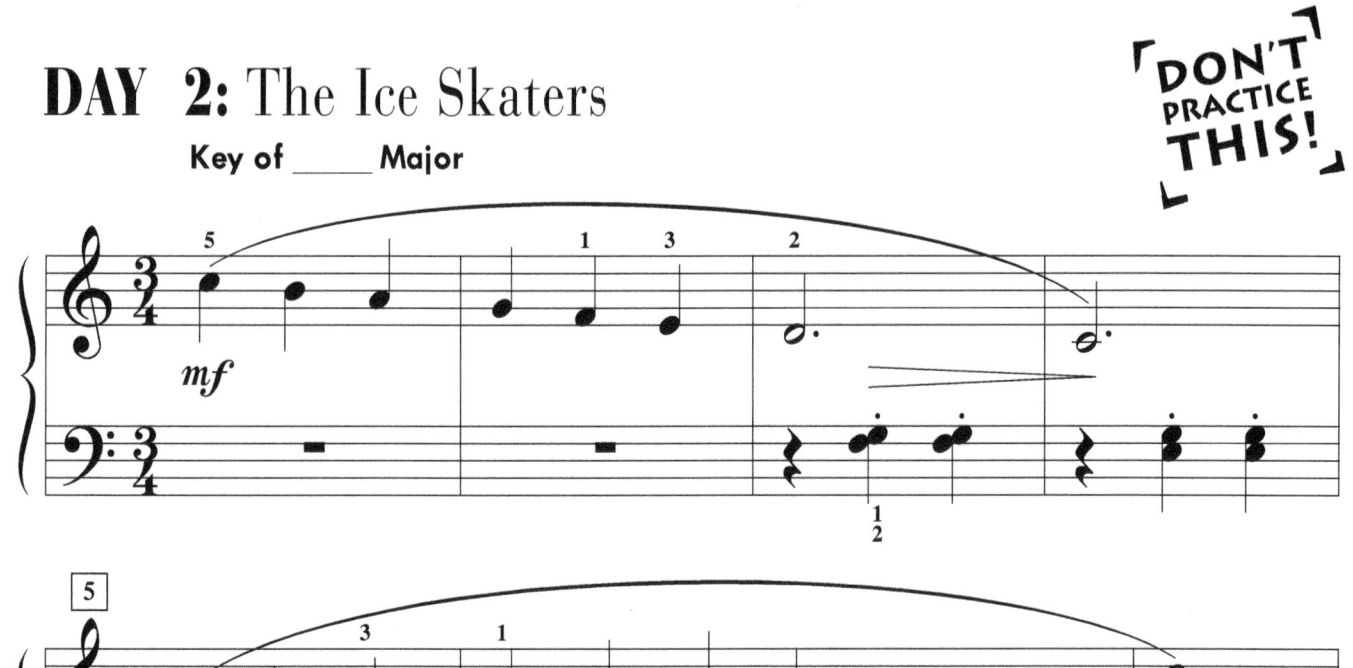

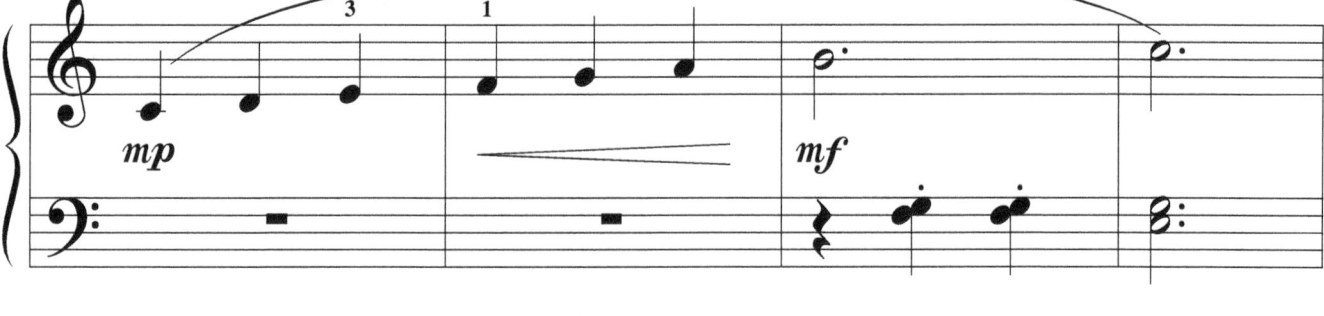

Connect each **scale step** to the skate that matches in the **key of C major**.

Scale Steps   Key of C Major

Draw **bar lines** in the music below.
Tap, counting "1 + 2 + 3 +".

DAY 3: The Ice Skaters

Key of _____ Major

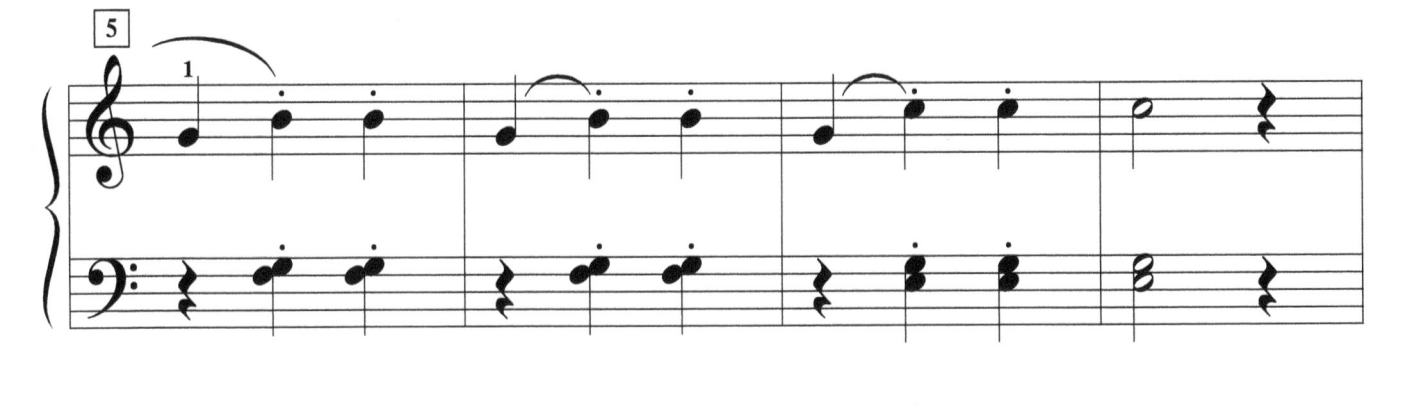

DAY 4: The Ice Skaters

Key of _____ Major

DON'T PRACTICE THIS!

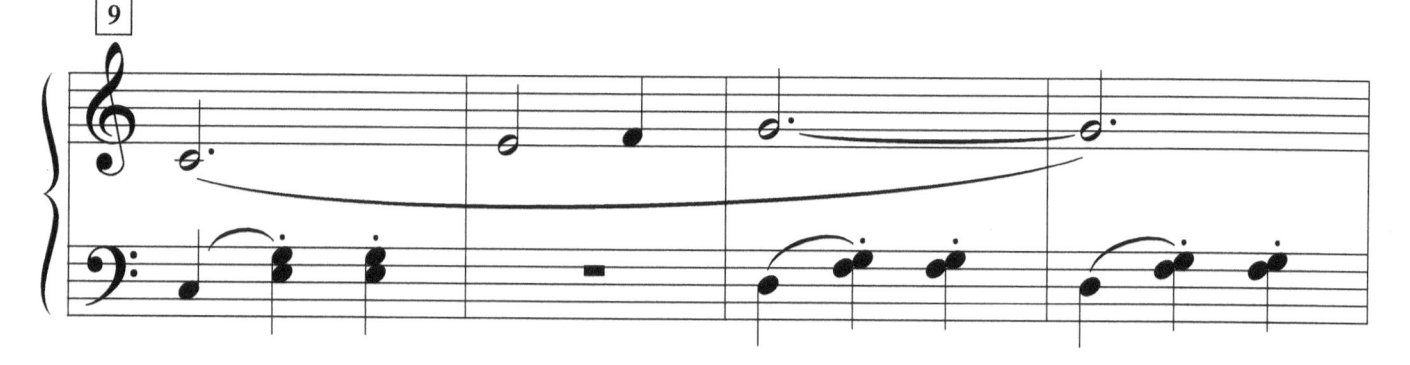

Write the three letter names of the C major chord in the skates.

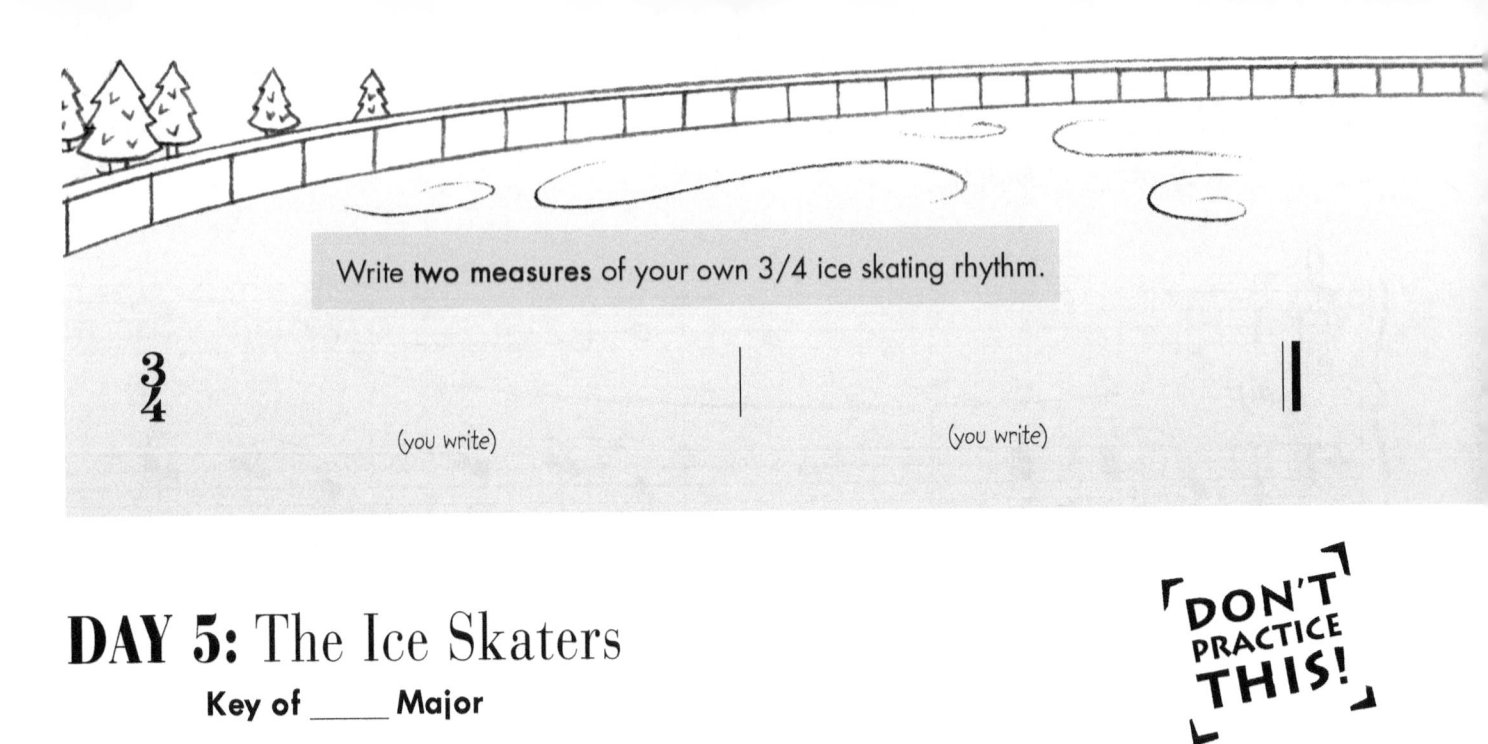

Write **two measures** of your own 3/4 ice skating rhythm.

(you write)　　　　　　　　(you write)

DAY 5: The Ice Skaters

Key of _____ Major

Count: 1 + 2 + 3

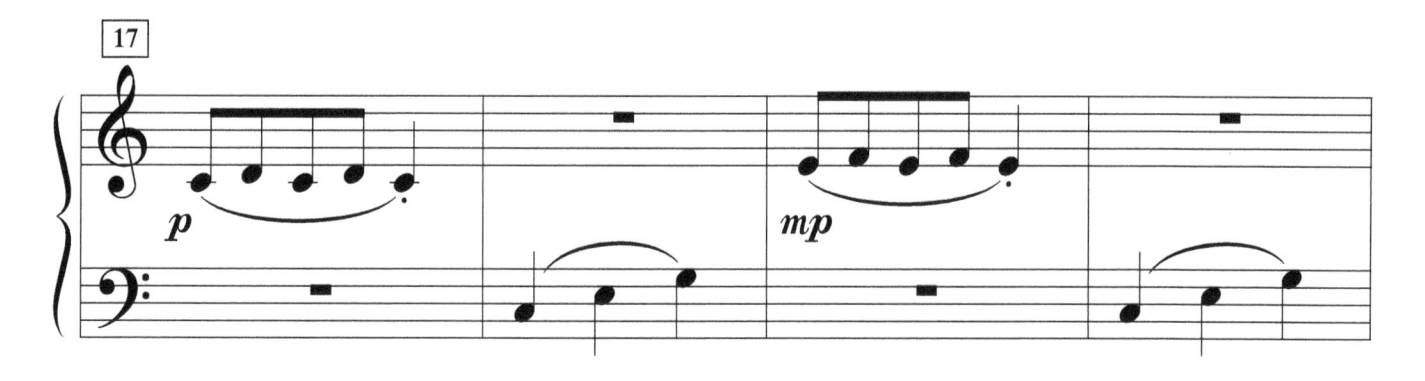

DAY 1: Vive la France!

Key of _____ Major

DON'T PRACTICE THIS!

Scan the music for F♯'s for each hand before playing.

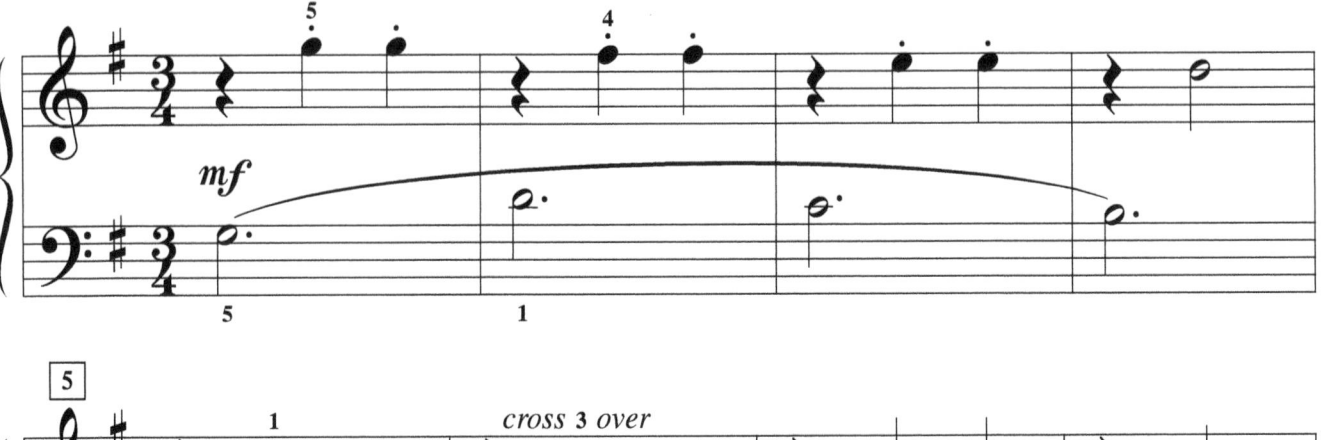

Circle the two correct **G major key signatures** above.

Circle the two signs that correctly spell the G major chord.

DAY 2: Vive la France!

Key of _____ Major

DON'T PRACTICE THIS!

Scan the music for F♯'s before playing.

Circle the notes that would be played as F♯ in the melody above. Hint: There are five.

DAY 3: Vive la France!

Key of _____ Major

DON'T PRACTICE THIS!

DAY 4: Vive la France!

Key of _____ Major

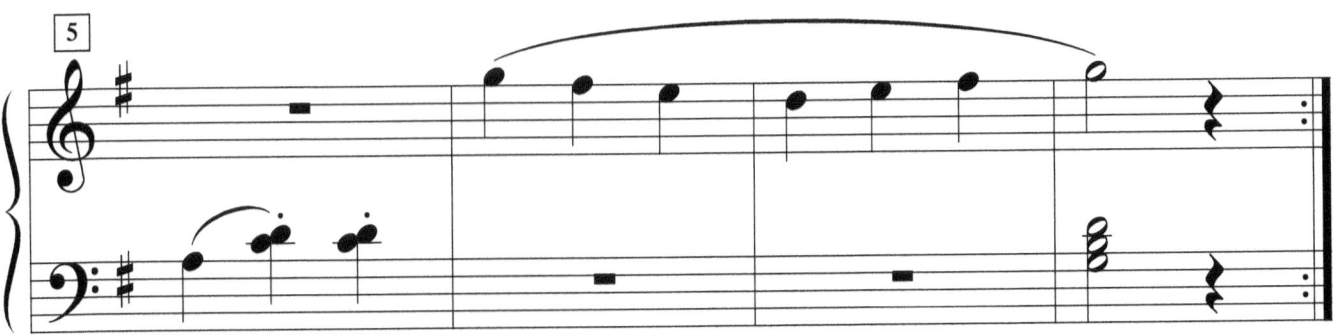

DAY 5: Vive la France!

Key of _____ Major

DON'T
PRACTICE
THIS!

Circle the letter sign that is the **tonic note** in the key of G major.

DAY 1: Horse-Drawn Carriage

Key of _____ Major

Scan the music for I and V7 chords.

Which measure begins with the **leading tone**? (scale step 7) measure _____ .

measure 7

Draw an X through the **incorrect measures.**

DAY 2: Horse-Drawn Carriage

Key of _____ Major

Count: 1 + 2 + 3 4

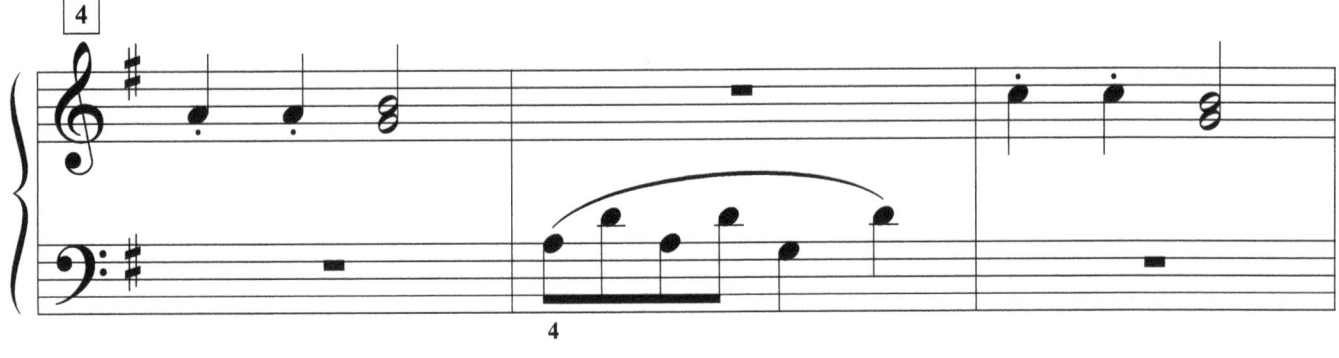

51

DAY 3: Horse-Drawn Carriage

Key of _____ Major

Scan the music. What two chords does the L.H. play?

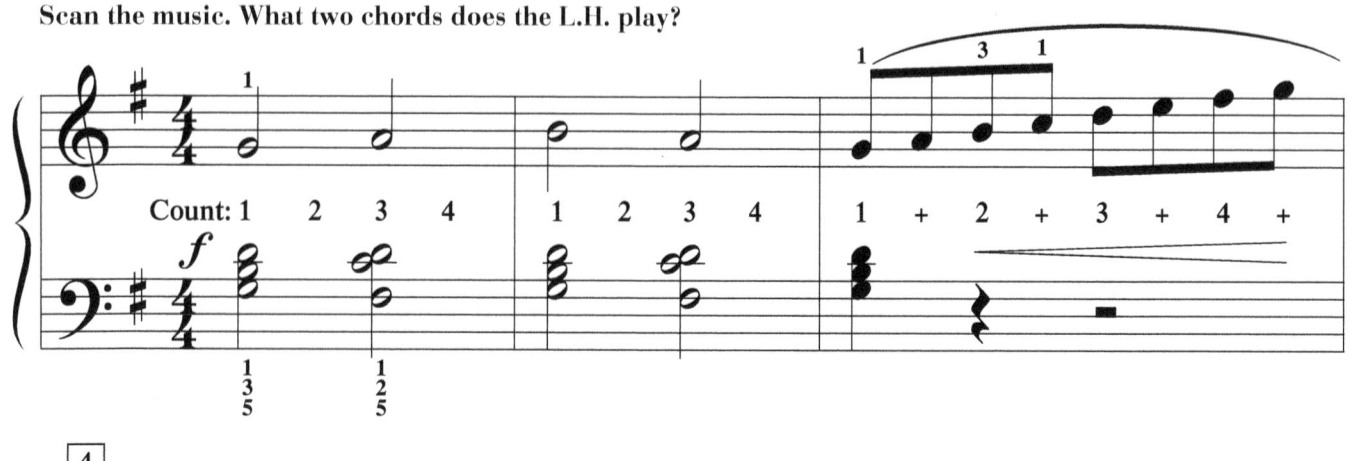

Write **one note** to equal the notes in each carriage.

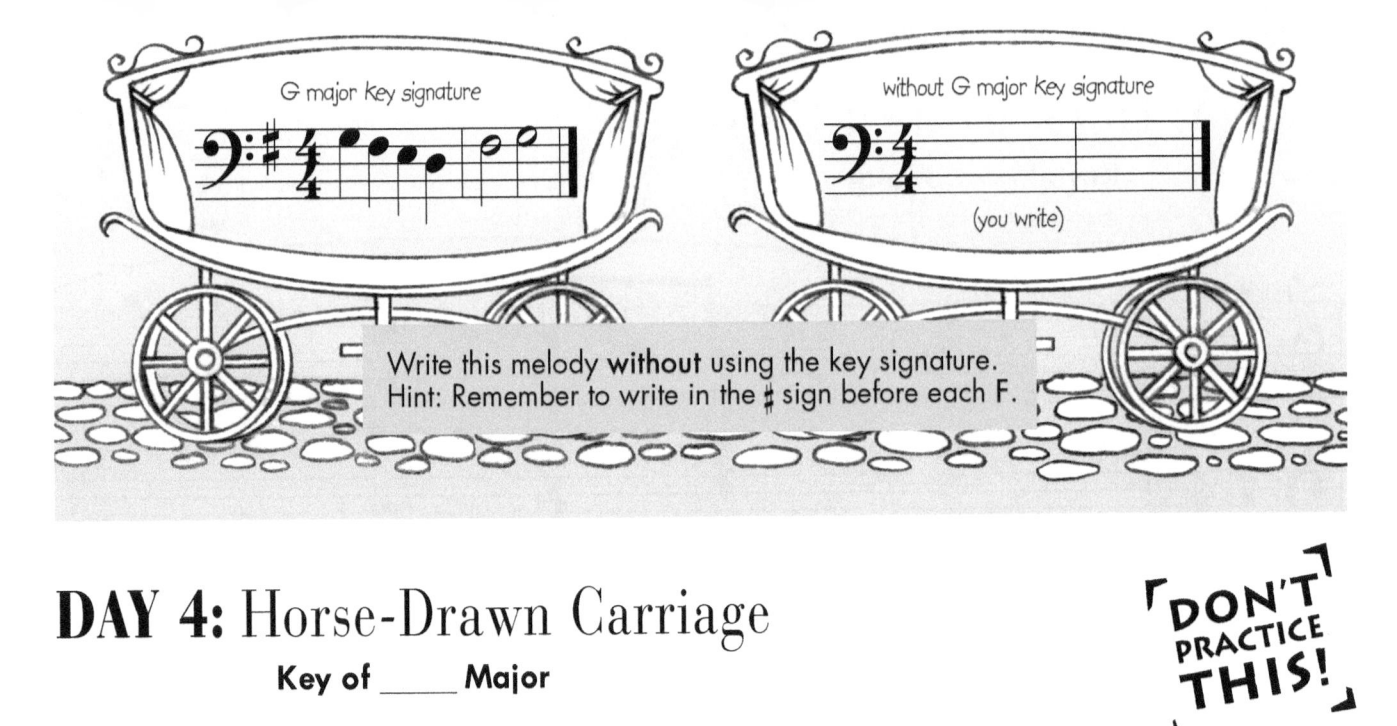

Write this melody **without** using the key signature.
Hint: Remember to write in the ♯ sign before each F.

DAY 4: Horse-Drawn Carriage

Key of _____ Major

DON'T
PRACTICE
THIS!

Notice this melody is for the L.H. alone.
Scan the music for F♯'s.

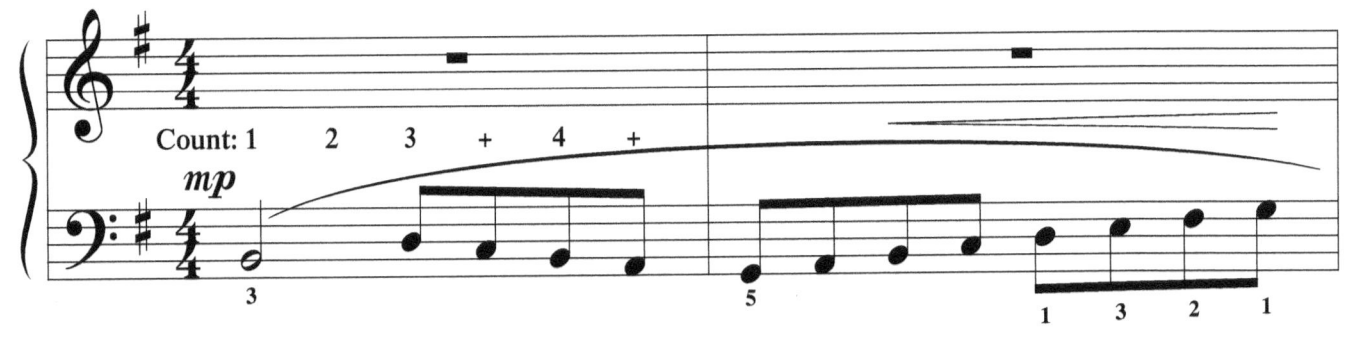

Count: 1   2   3   +   4   +

mp

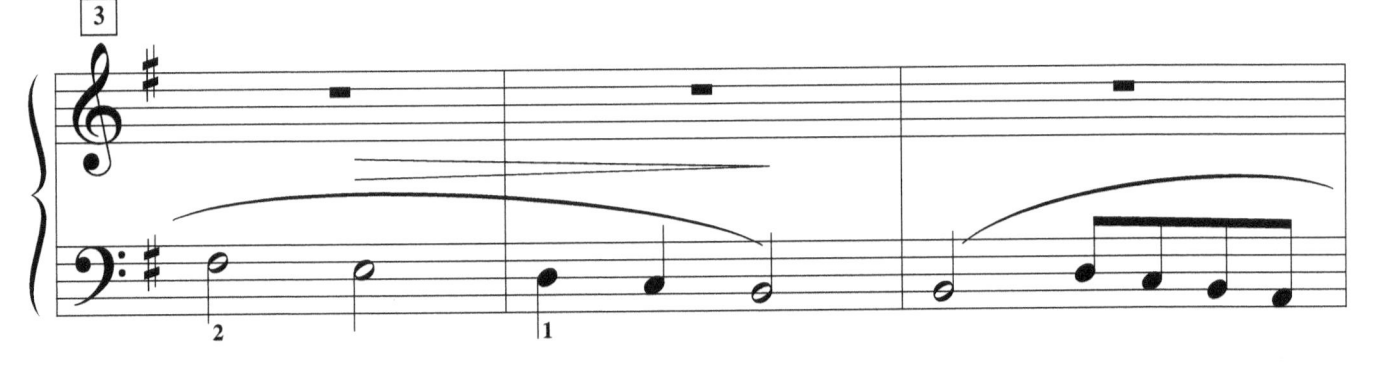

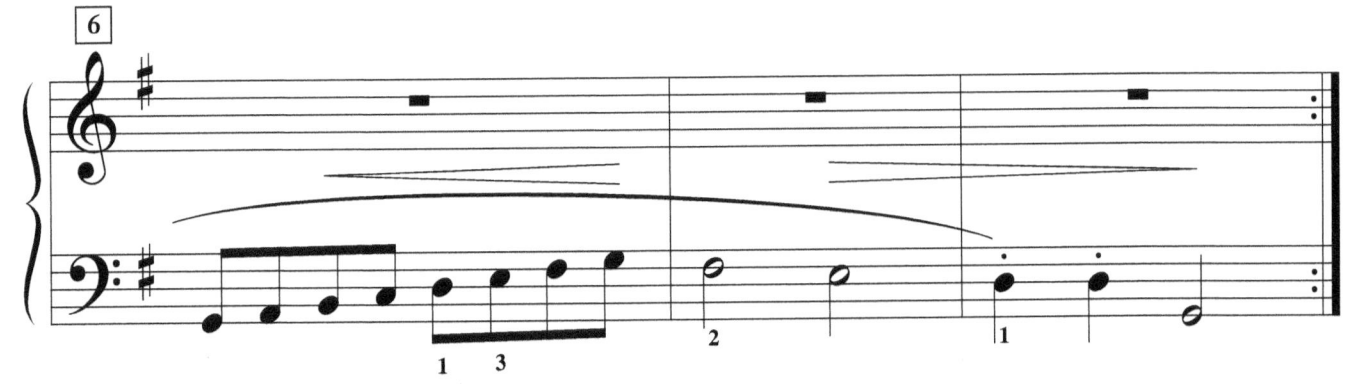

53

DAY 5: Horse-Drawn Carriage

Key of _____ Major

Draw **one rest** in each measure to match the time signature.

Quarter rest   Half rest   Whole rest

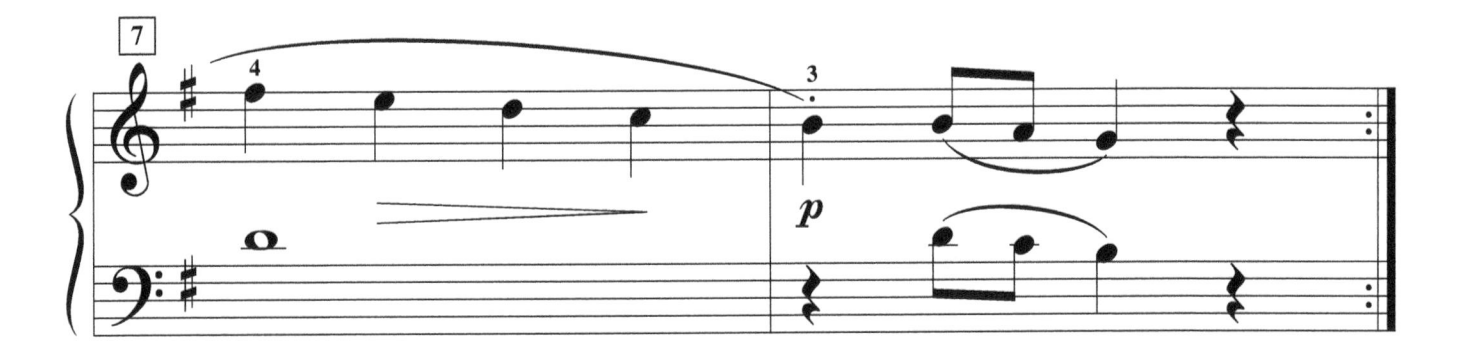

mf – mp on repeat

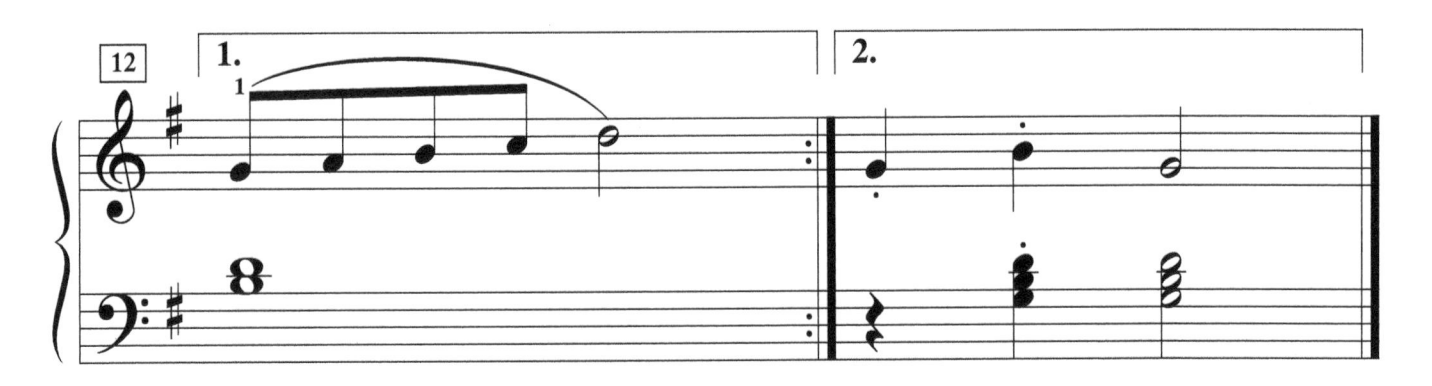

DAY 1: Beach Party

Key of _____ Major

Notice the R.H. shifts from C major down to A minor chords.
Plan how you will play them!

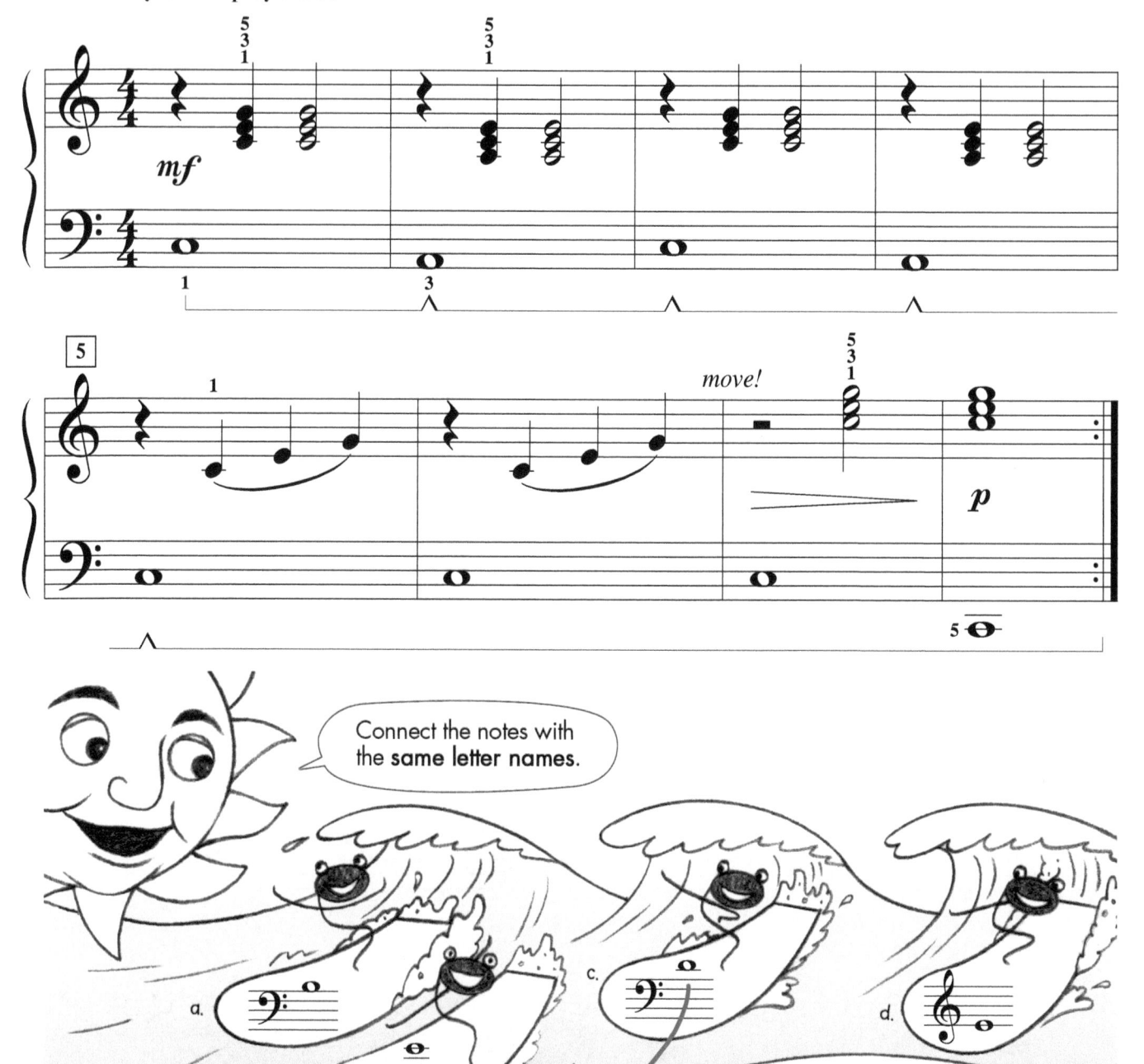

Connect the notes with the **same letter names**.

Example

56

Connect each **chord symbol** to the matching **broken chord** on the staff.

DAY 2: Beach Party

Key of _____ Major

DON'T PRACTICE THIS!

Scan the music. The R.H. makes four shifts. Can you spot them all?

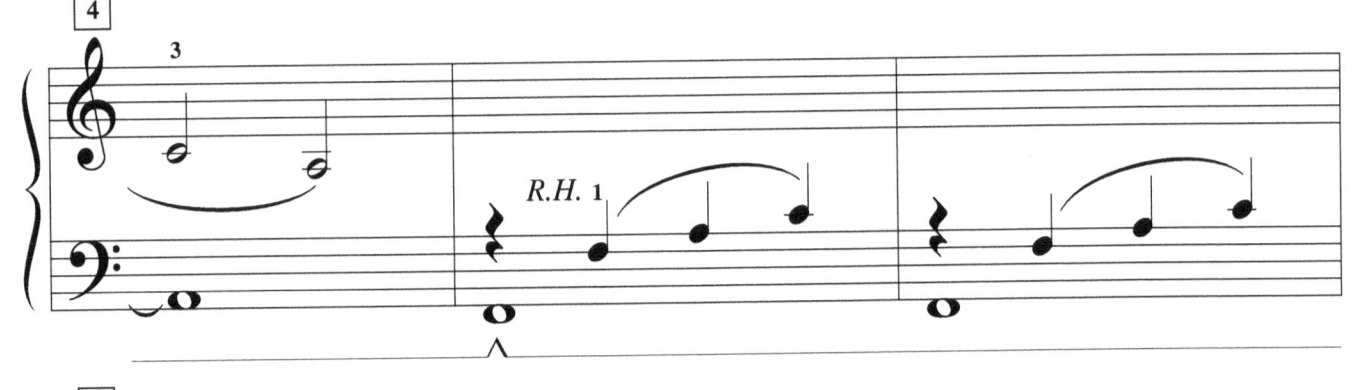

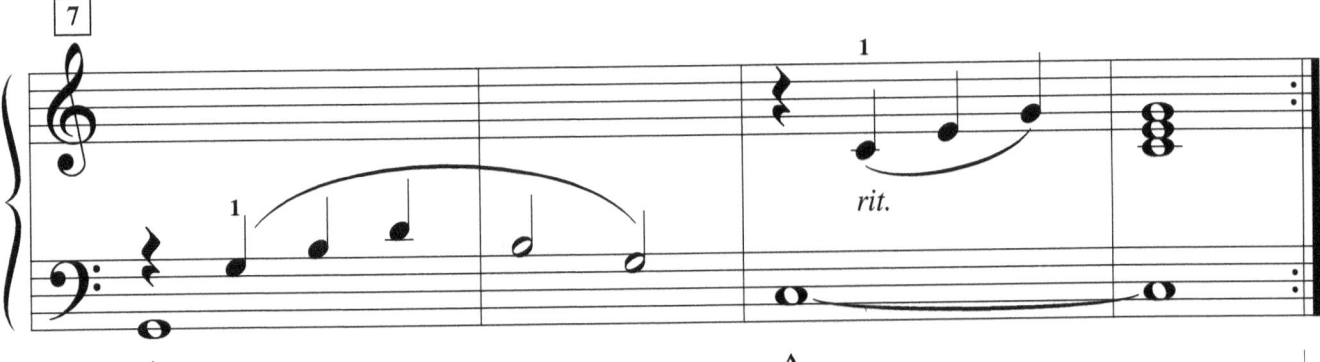

DAY 3: Beach Party

Key of _____ Major

Scan the hand shifts for the R.H. before sightreading.

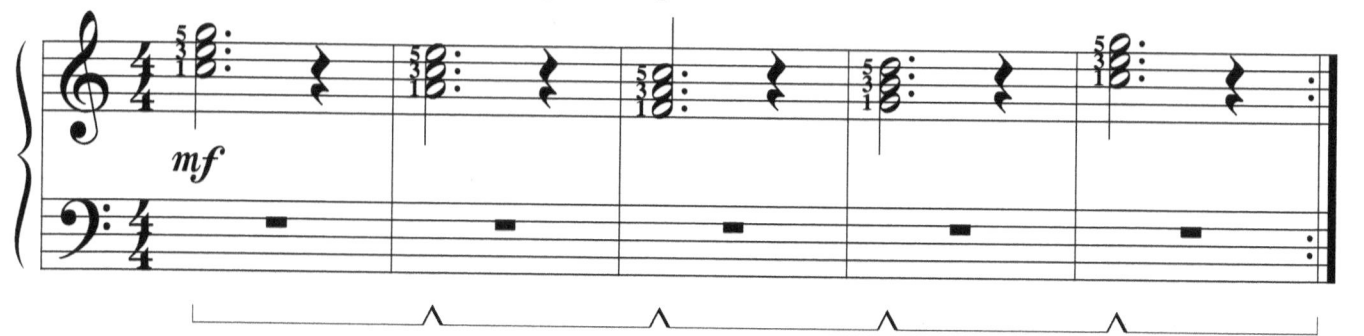

DAY 4: Beach Party

Key of _____ Major

Spell the **chords** on each surfboard from bottom to top.

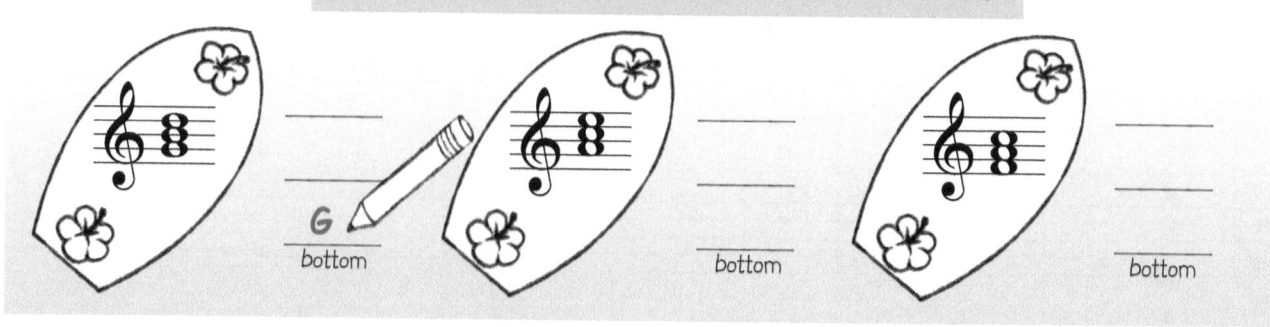

58

How many times does this 4/4 rhythm occur? _____ times.

DAY 5: Beach Party

Key of _____ Major

Scan the hand shifts for the R.H. before sightreading.

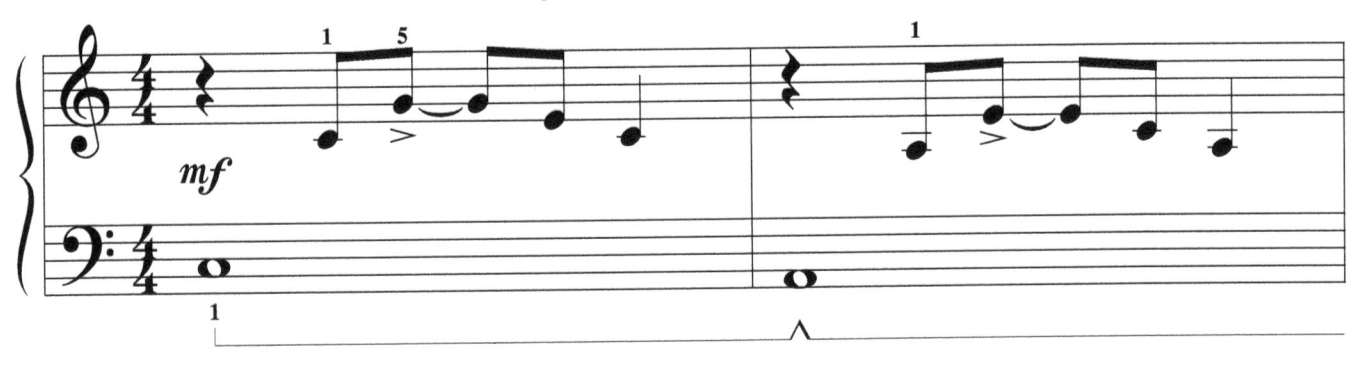

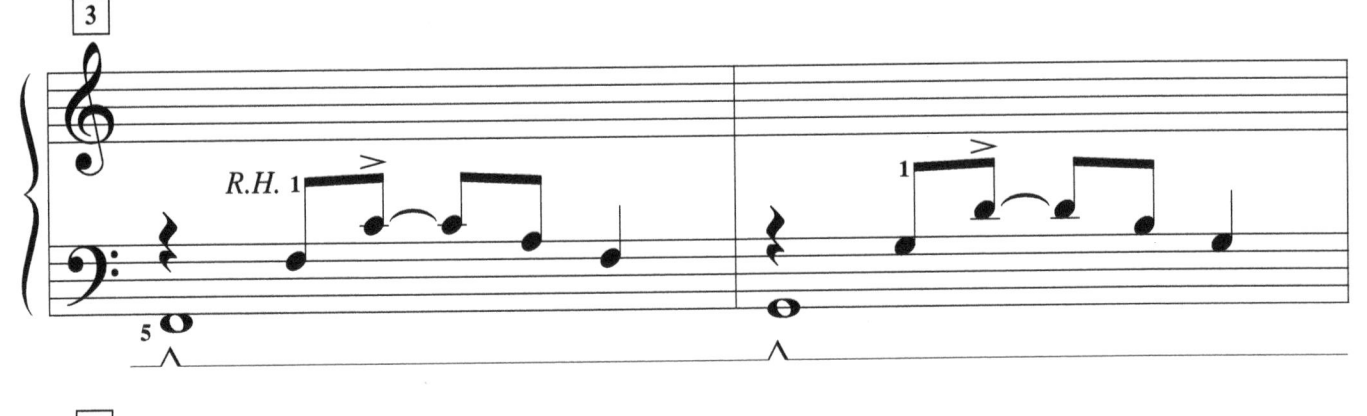

DAY 1: Pumpkin Boogie

Key of C Minor

Hint: Find the hardest measures before sightreading.
Silently play or think these measures in your head.
Which measures did you choose?

Name the **highest** note in this piece. ___

Name the **lowest** note in this piece. ___

Which note uses a **flat**? ___

60

Name the **intervals** in the pumpkin patch.

2nd

DAY 2: Pumpkin Boogie
Key of C Minor

DON'T PRACTICE THIS!

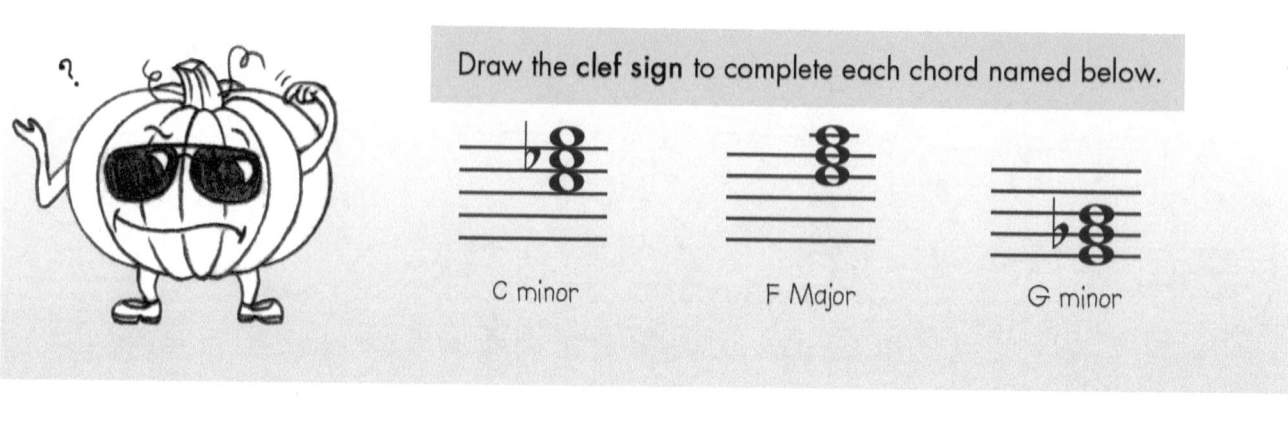

Draw the **clef sign** to complete each chord named below.

C minor   F Major   G minor

DAY 3: Pumpkin Boogie
Key of C Minor

DON'T PRACTICE THIS!

Scan the music and notice the L.H. fingering.

DAY 4: Pumpkin Boogie
Key of C Minor

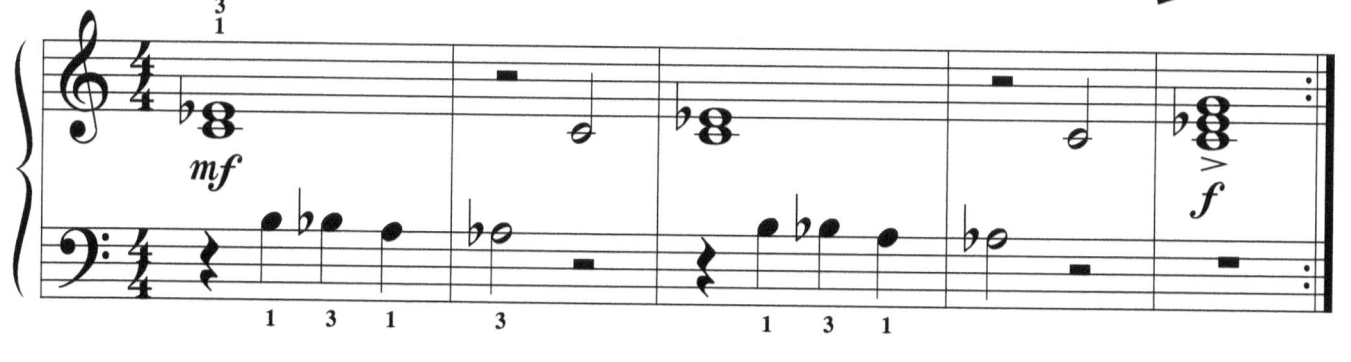

DAY 5: Pumpkin Boogie

Key of C Minor

Scan the music. What two chords does the L.H. play?

RHYTHM ROAD — Write **two measures** of 4/4 rhythm. Use at least one **eighth rest**.

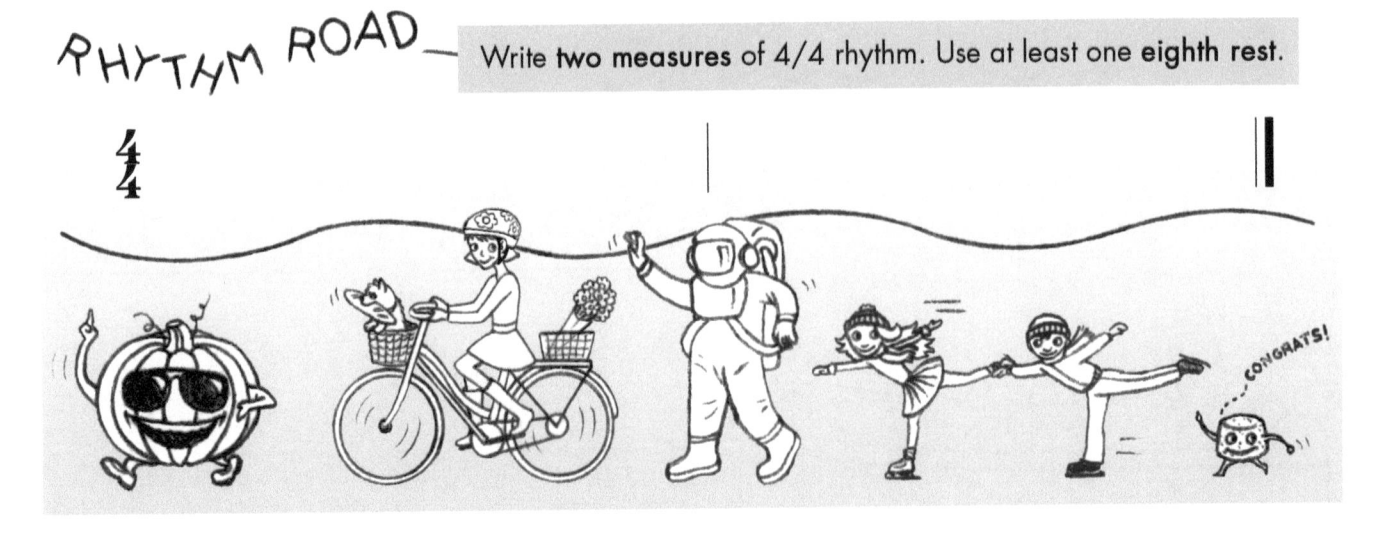

DAY 1: Deck the Keys

Key of _____ Major

Notice the ♩. is always followed by a single ♪ note.
Feel the dot on beat 2!

Count: 1 2 + 3 4   1 2 3 4

Connect the rhythms with the **same number of beats**.

64

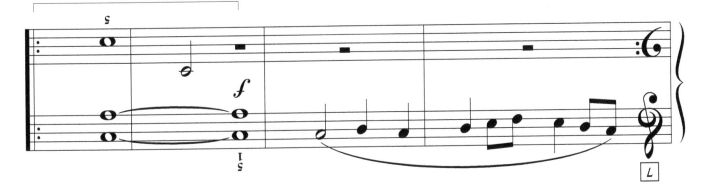

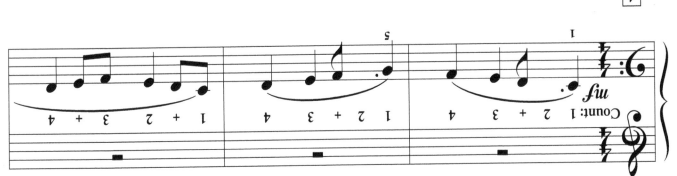

DON'T PRACTICE THIS!

DAY 2: Deck the Keys

Key of _____ Major

Scan the music. Notice the ♩. ♪ rhythm pattern.
Feel the dot on beat 2!

How many measures in DAY 2
use this rhythm pattern?
2, 3, 4, or 5 (circle one)

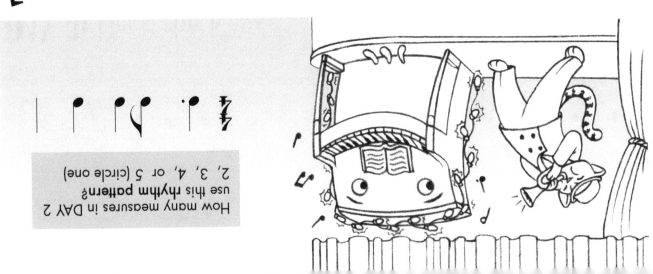

DAY 3: Deck the Keys

Key of _____ Major

DON'T PRACTICE THIS!

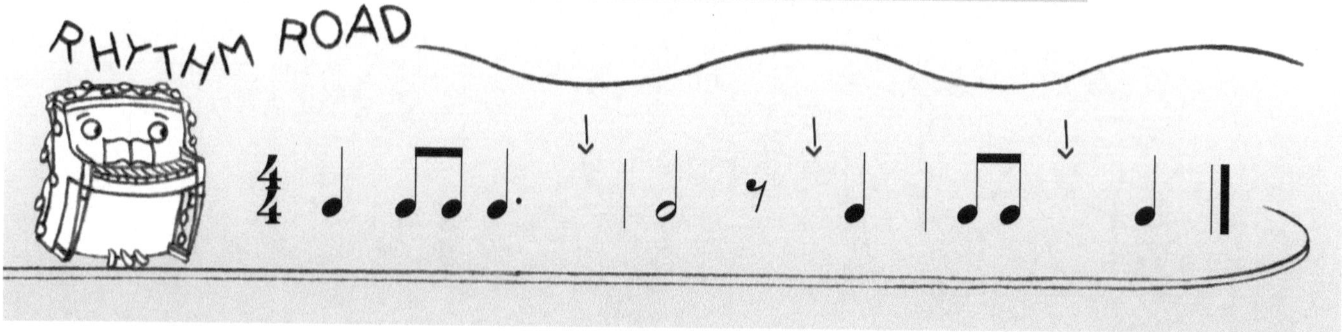

Scan the music. Do you see a rhythm pattern?

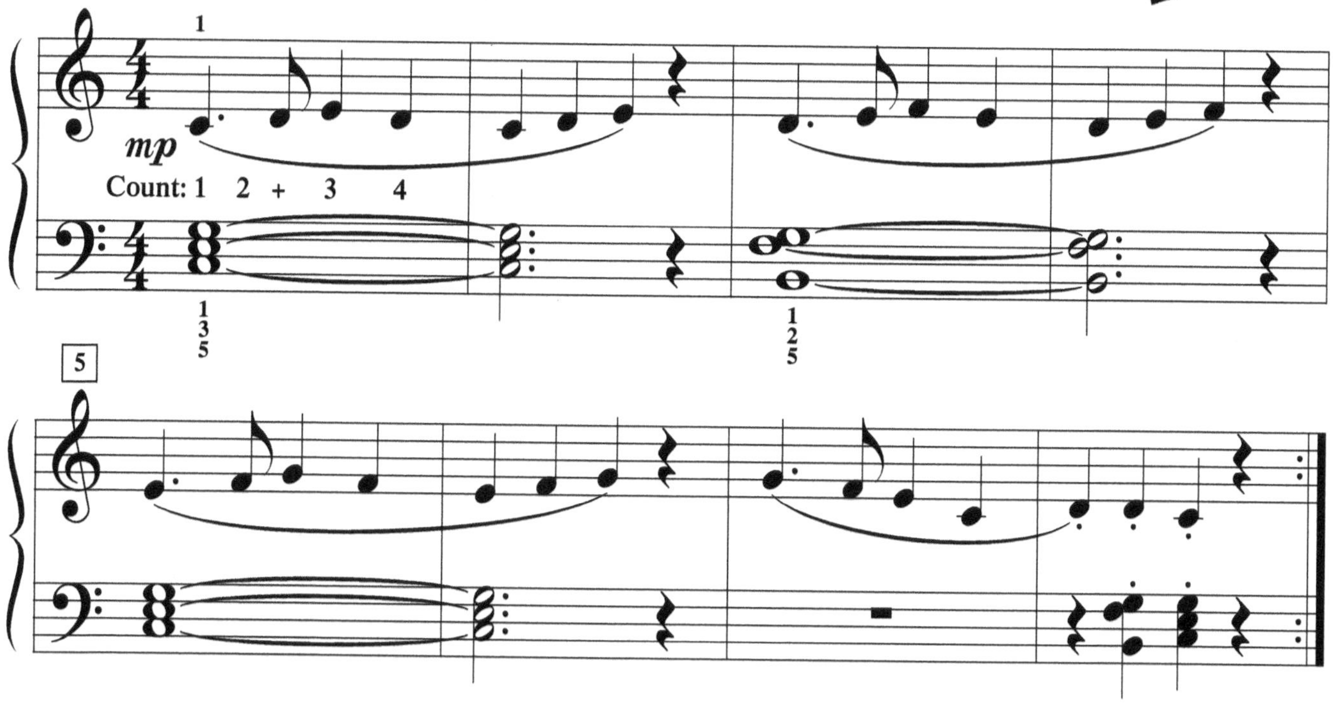

Count: 1   2   +   3   4

DAY 4: Deck the Keys

Key of _____ Major

Hint: Feel the quarter rests in measure 4.

DAY 5: Deck the Keys

Key of _____ Major

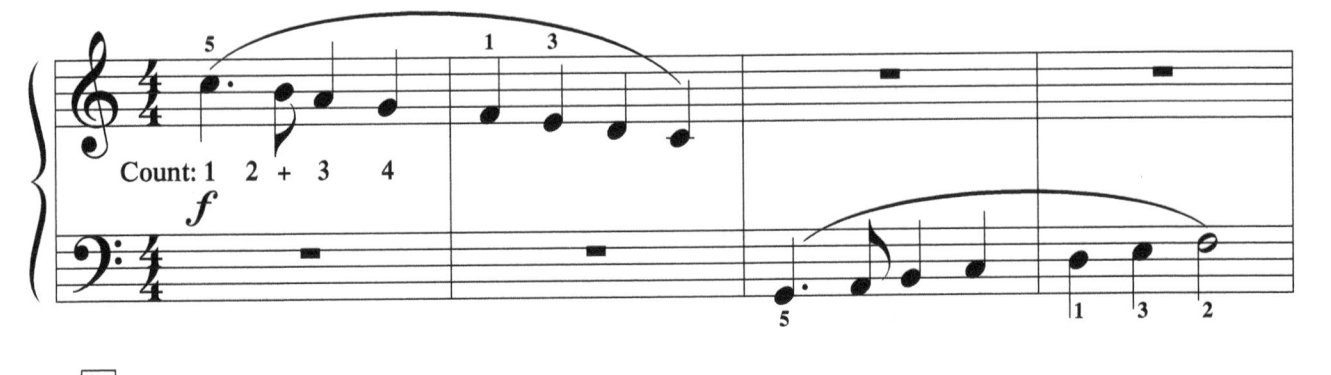

Count: 1   2   +   3   4

Write **one measure** of the hardest rhythm you can think of in 4/4 time.

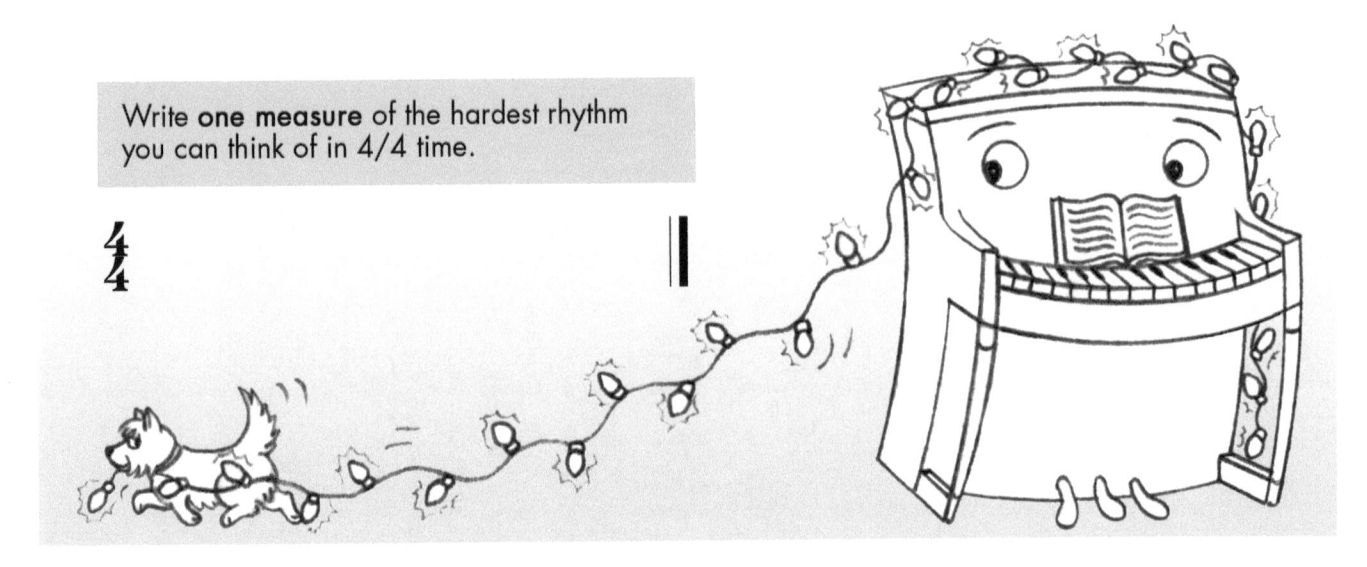

DAY 1: This Is My Planet Earth

Key of _____ Major

DON'T PRACTICE THIS!

Name the **bass clef lines,** lowest to highest.

Name the **treble clef lines,** lowest to highest.

68

Draw the following notes in the stars.

quarter note

half note

eighth note

dotted quarter note

whole note

dotted half note

DAY 2: This Is My Planet Earth

Key of _____ Major

DON'T PRACTICE THIS!

Hint: Prepare your L.H. before starting.

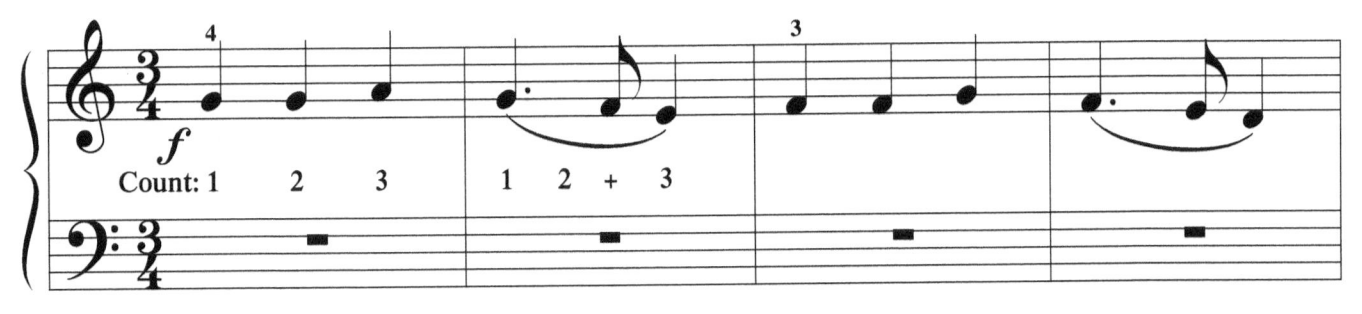

Count: 1   2   3   1   2   +   3

DAY 3: This Is My Planet Earth

Key of _____ Major

Count: 1   2   +   3   + | 1   2   +   3

cross over

DAY 4: This Is My Planet Earth

Key of _____ Major

Count: 1   2   +   3   + | 1   2   +   3

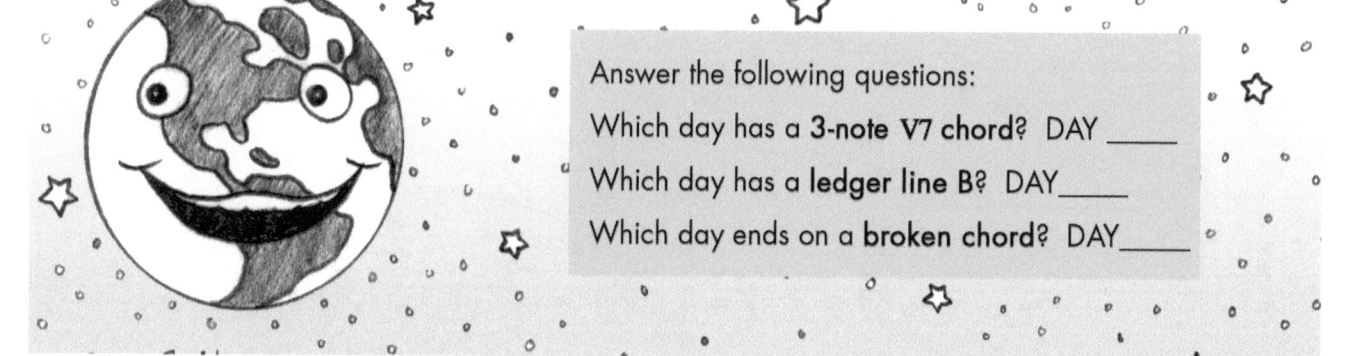

Answer the following questions:

Which day has a **3-note V7 chord?** DAY _____

Which day has a **ledger line B?** DAY_____

Which day ends on a **broken chord?** DAY_____

Name the **intervals** floating in outer space.

DAY 5: This Is My Planet Earth

Key of _____ Major

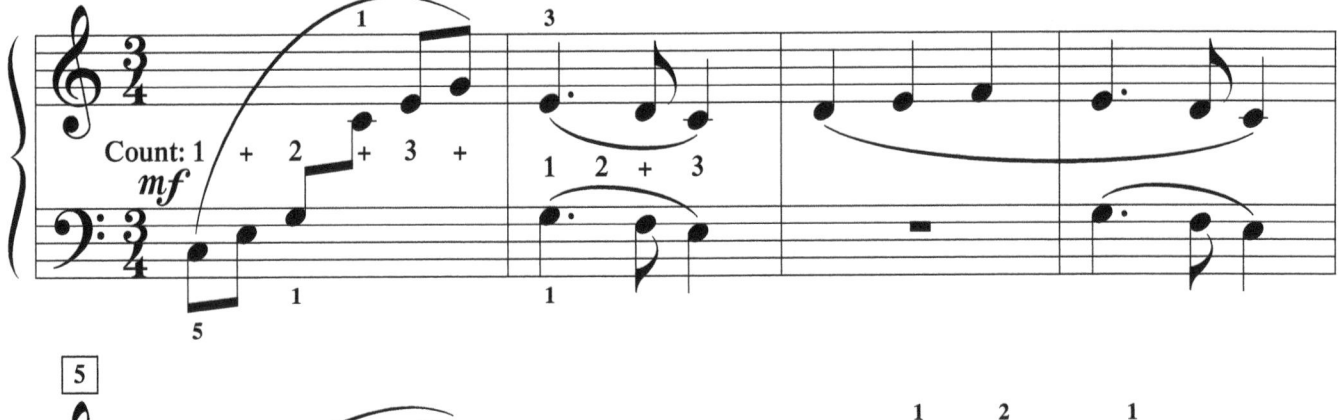

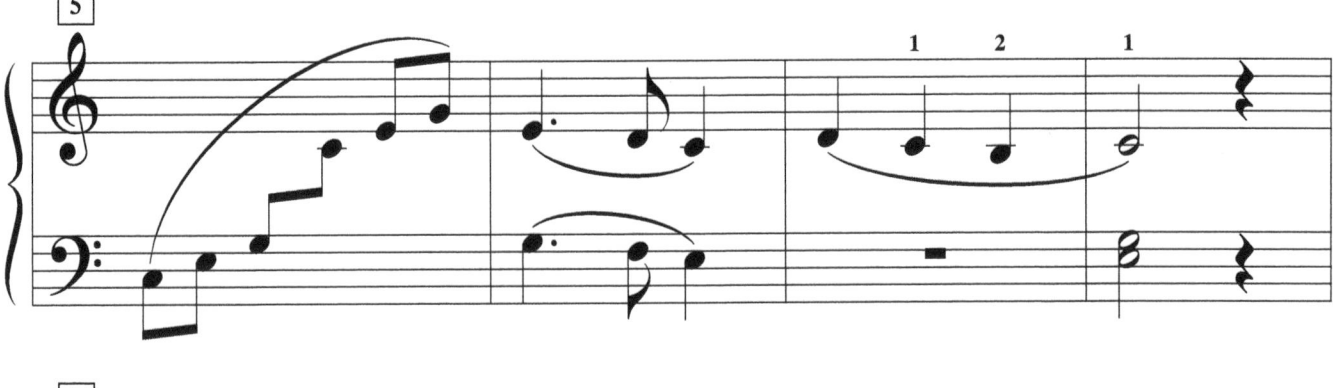

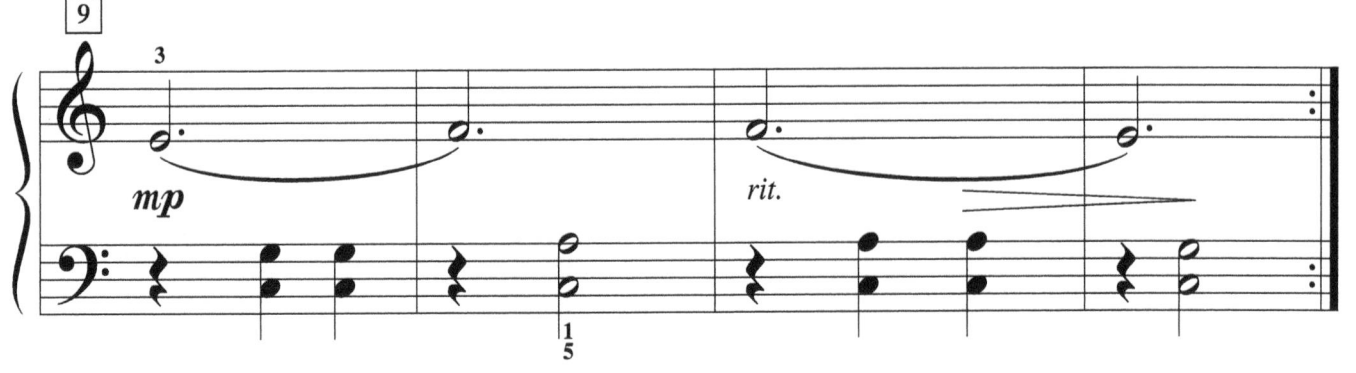

How many measures contain the **IV chord** in the key of C major? (circle one)

1, 2, 3, or 4

DAY 1: Lazy Chord Blues

Key of ____ Major

DON'T
PRACTICE
THIS!

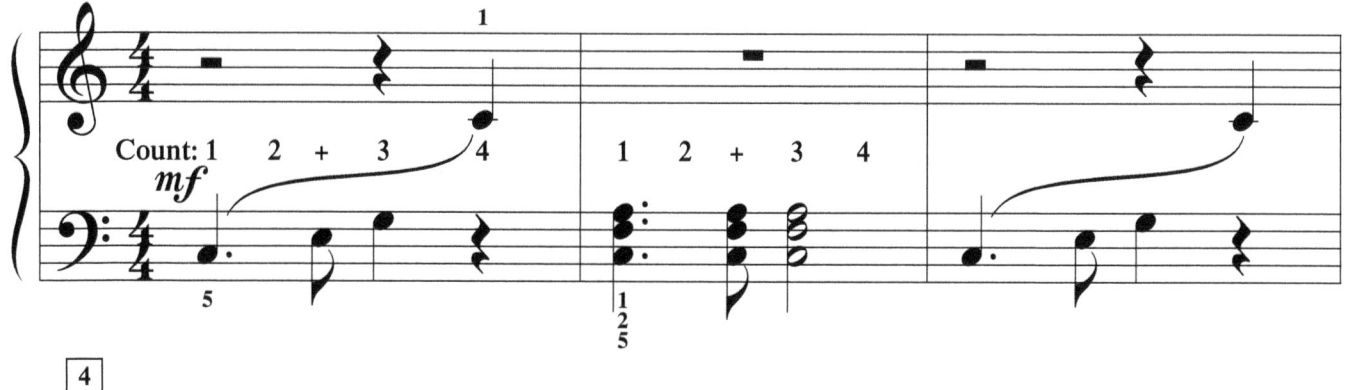

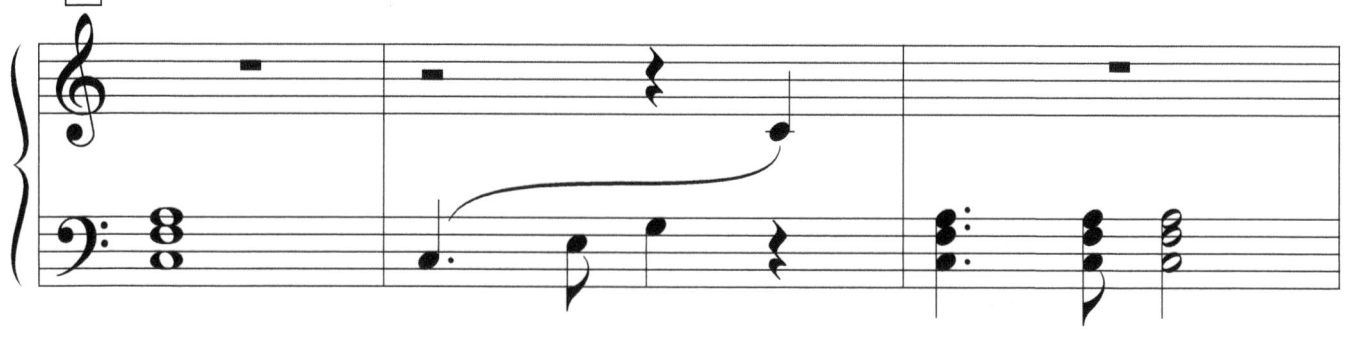

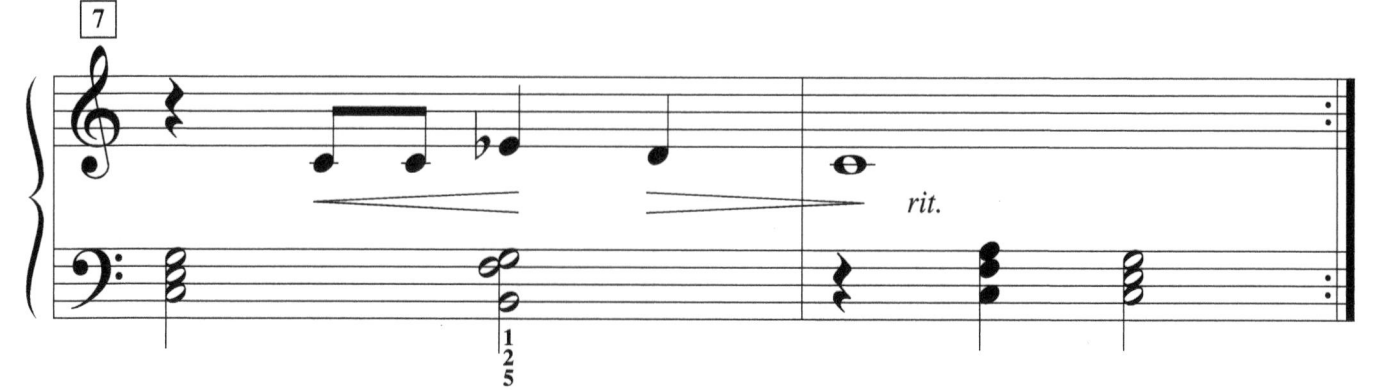

DAY 2: Lazy Chord Blues

Key of _____ Major

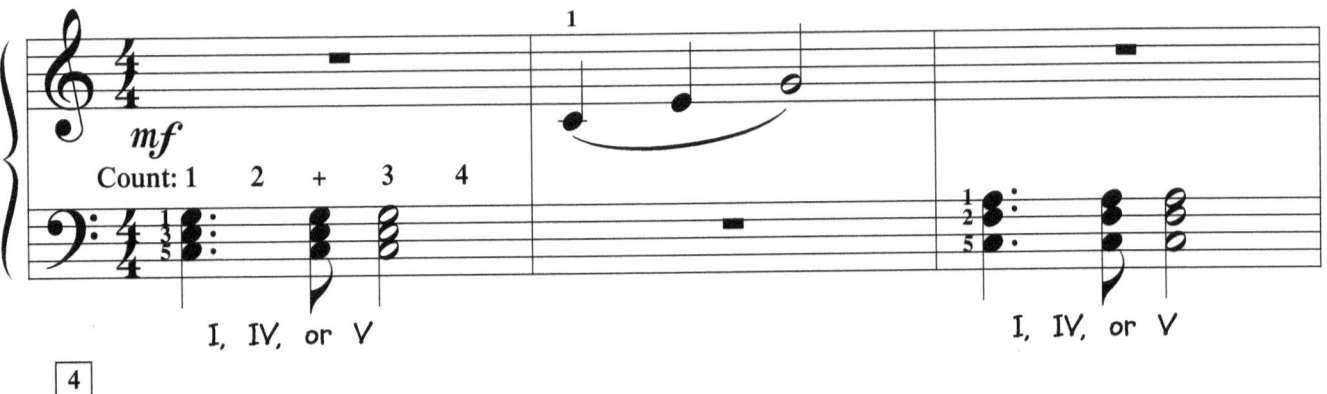

Count: 1   2   +   3   4

I, IV, or V   I, IV, or V

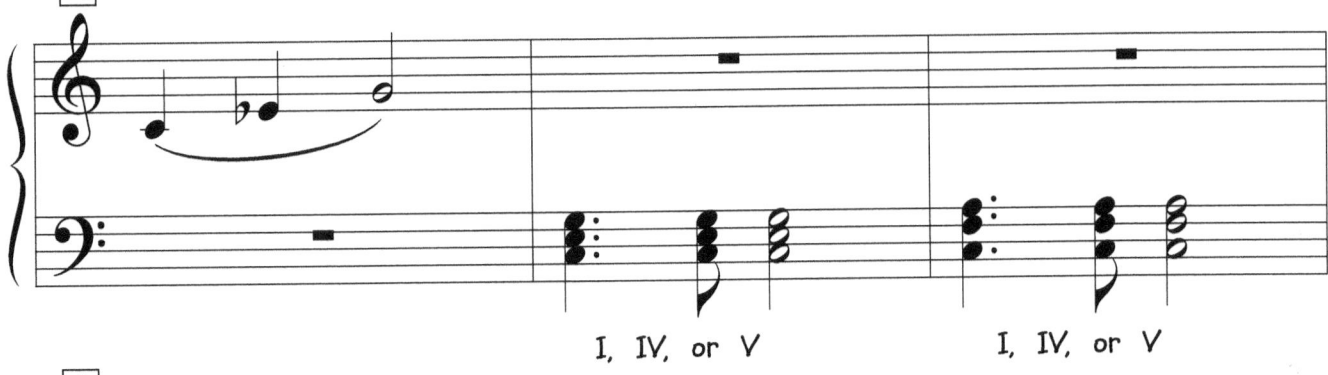

I, IV, or V   I, IV, or V

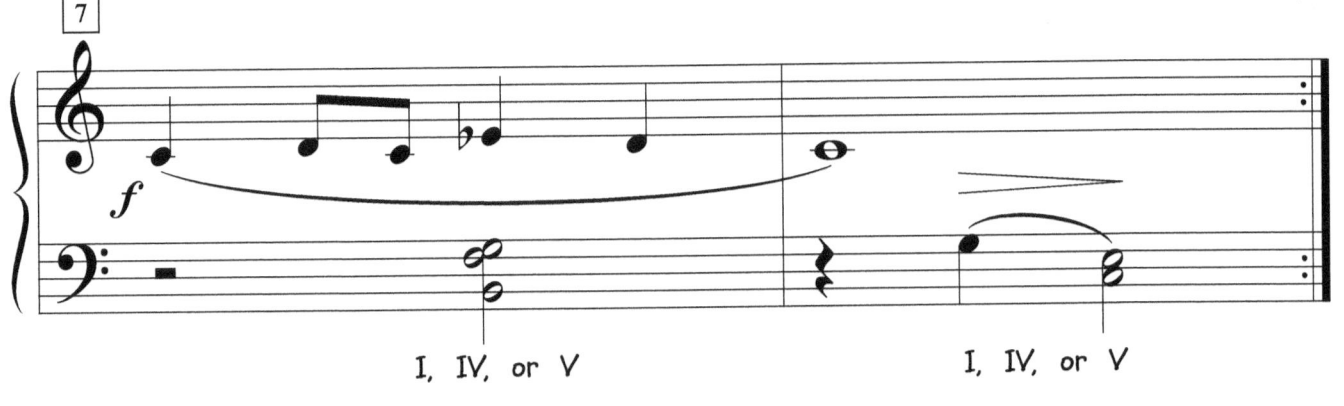

I, IV, or V   I, IV, or V

Circle the correct **chord symbol** for the measures above.

DAY 3: Lazy Chord Blues
Key of _____ Major

Count: 1 2 3 4   1 2 + 3 4

DAY 4: Lazy Chord Blues
Key of _____ Major

Hint: Does the L.H. begin on the I, IV, or V7 chord?

Count: 1 + 2 + 3 4   1 2 + 3 4

Name the **accidental** in DAY 1. ___
Name the **accidental** in DAY 2. ___

CONGRATS!
This music uses **two chords**. What are they?
_____ and _____.

DAY 5: Lazy Chord Blues

Key of _____ Major

DON'T PRACTICE **THIS!**

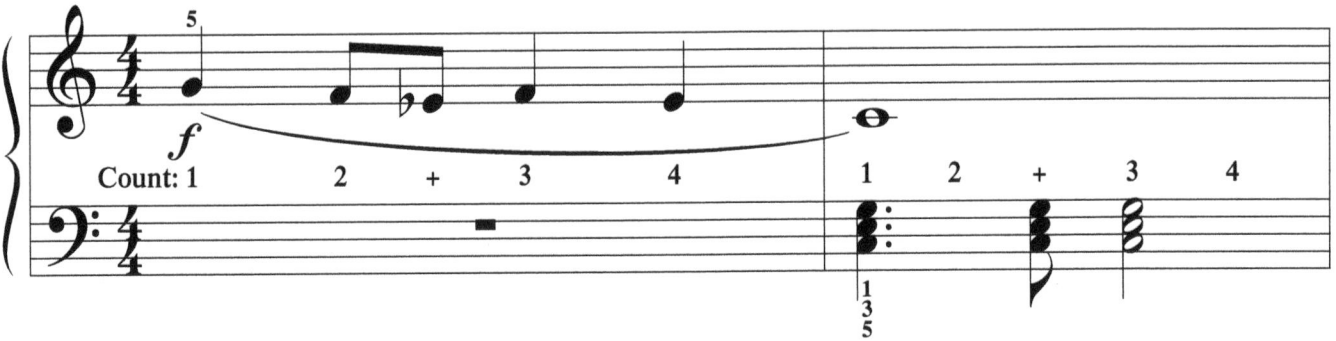

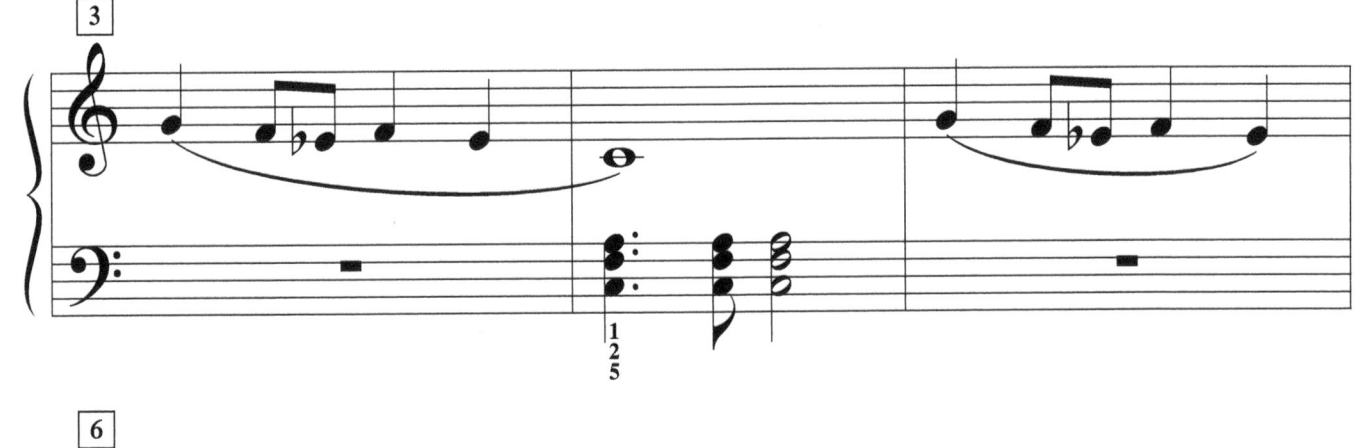

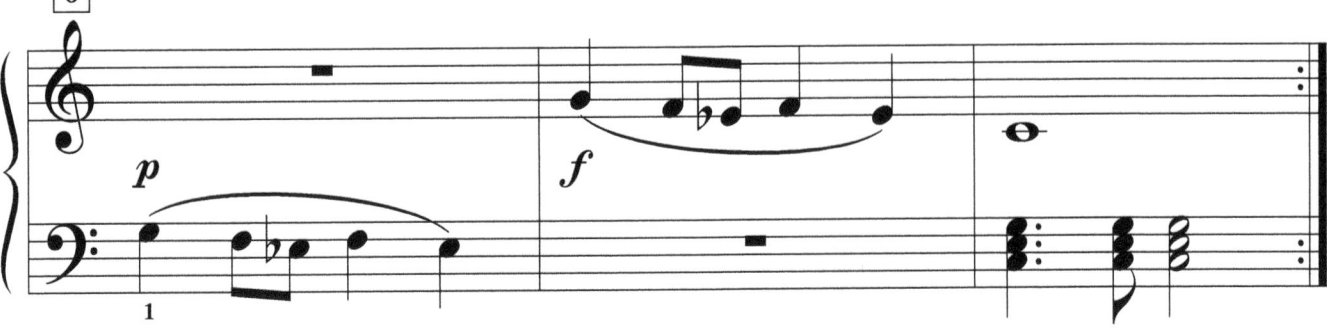

DAY 2: Duke of York Strut

Key of _____ Major

DON'T
PRACTICE
THIS!

Circle the correctly labeled chord examples.
Draw an X through the incorrect examples.

DAY 3: Duke of York Strut

Key of _____ Major

Count: 1 + 2 + 3 4

DAY 4: Duke of York Strut

Key of _____ Major

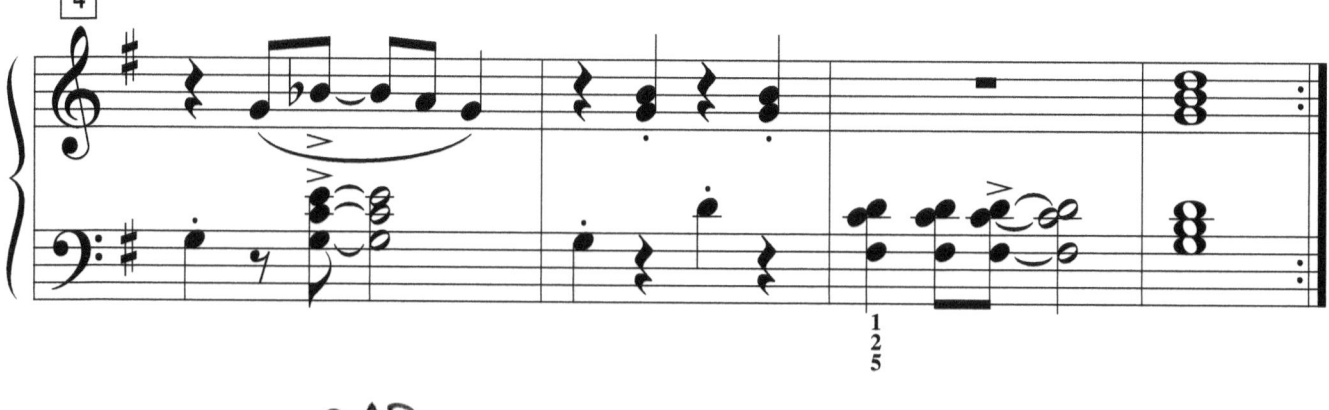

RHYTHM ROAD

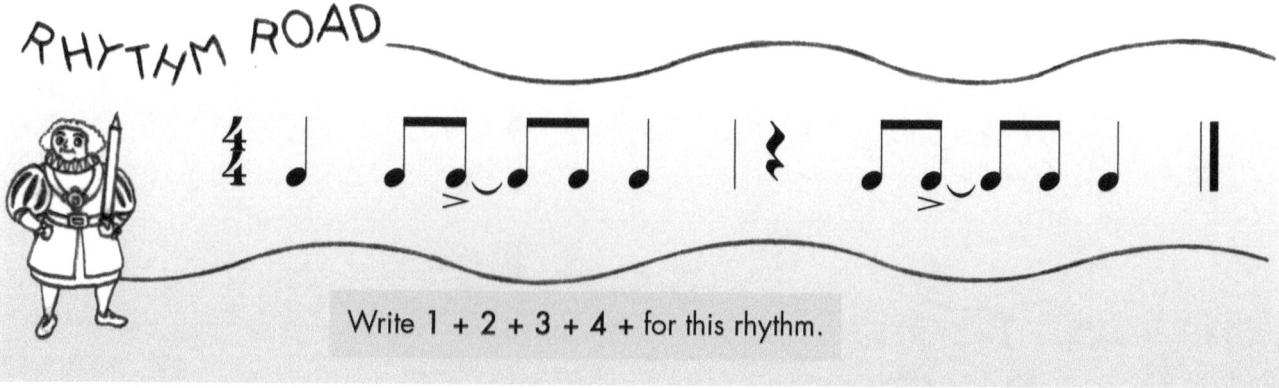

Write 1 + 2 + 3 + 4 + for this rhythm.

78

Write the **letter names** of the G major scale. Include any sharps.

Letter names: _G_ _ _ _ _ _ _ _

CONGRATULATIONS

DAY 5: Duke of York Strut

Key of _____ Major

DON'T PRACTICE THIS!

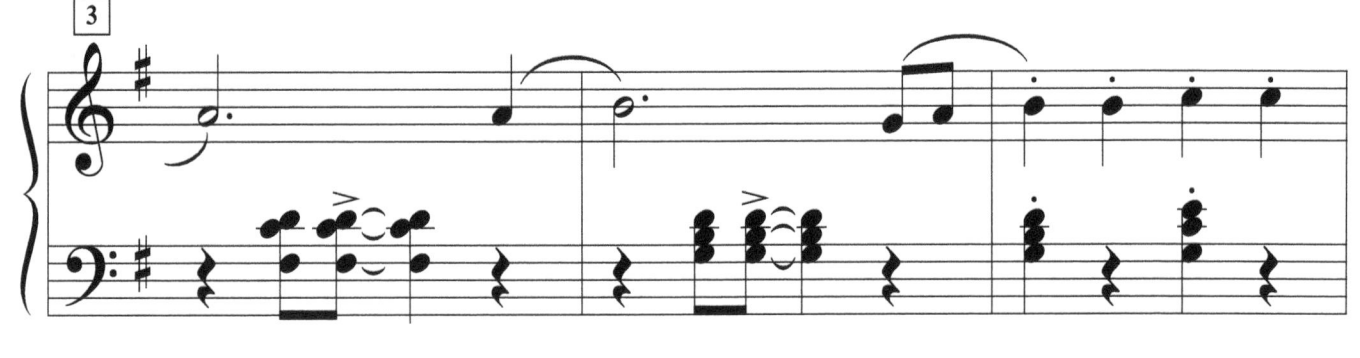

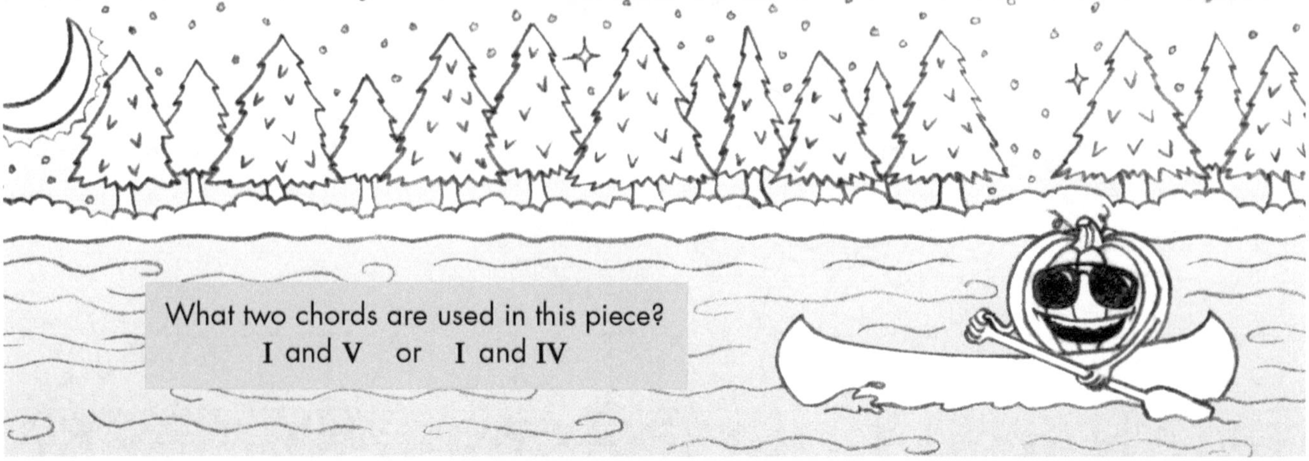

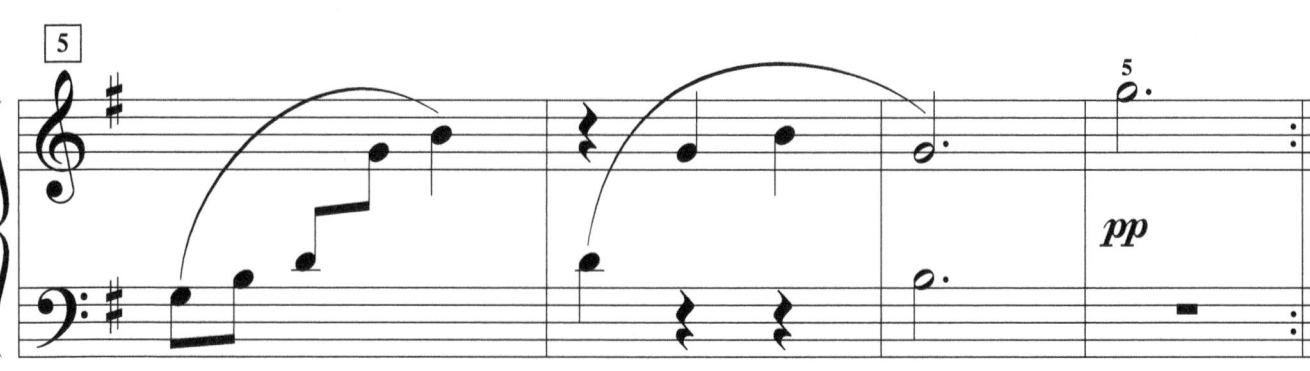

What two chords are used in this piece?
I and V   or   I and IV

DAY 1: Canoeing in the Moonlight

Key of _____ Major

Find the location of the last note before you begin.

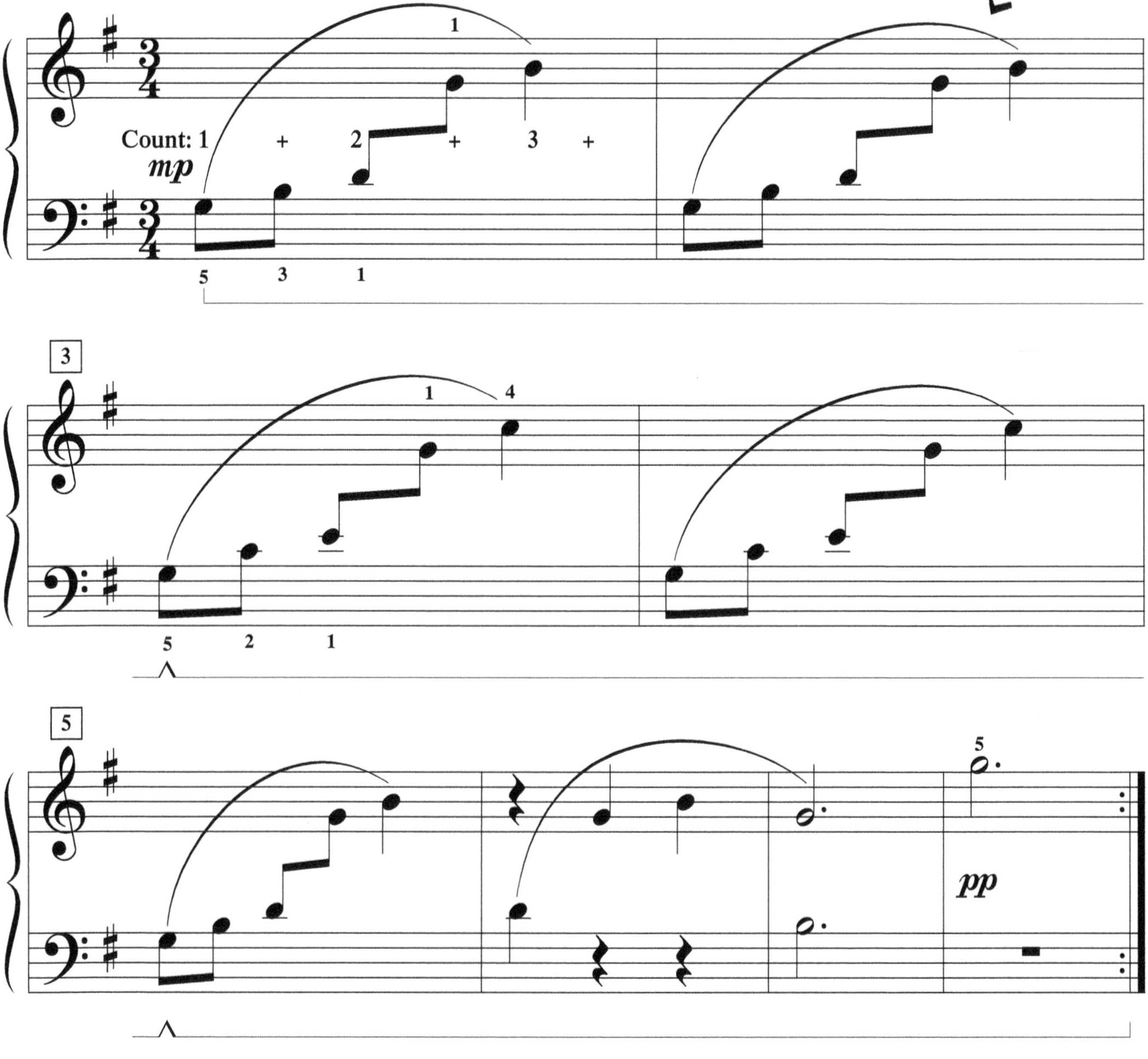

Count: 1   +   2   +   3   +

mp

5   3   1

pp

DAY 2: Canoeing in the Moonlight

Key of _____ Major

Find the location of the last note before you begin.

Count: 1   2   +   3

mp

pp

What does the number 4 in the **time signature** mean?

_____

_____

DAY 3: Canoeing in the Moonlight

Key of _____ Major

Write **1 + 2 + 3 +** under the correct beats.

Write the **scale step** of each note in the key of G major. Notice the clef sign.

DAY 4: Canoeing in the Moonlight
Key of _____ Major

DON'T PRACTICE THIS!

Hint: Prepare the R.H. fingers over the correct notes before starting.

DAY 5: Canoeing in the Moonlight

Key of _____ Major

DON'T PRACTICE THIS!

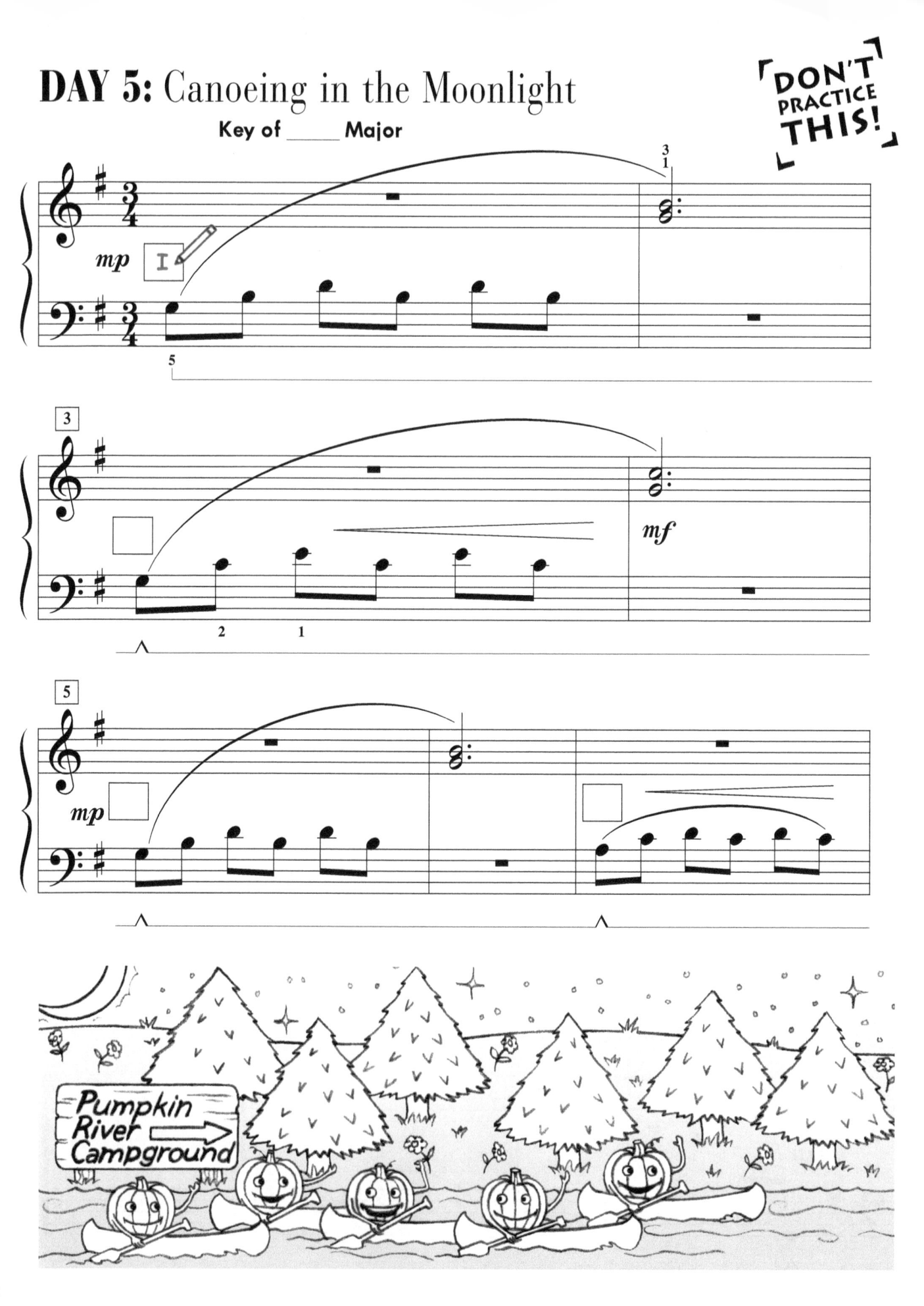

84

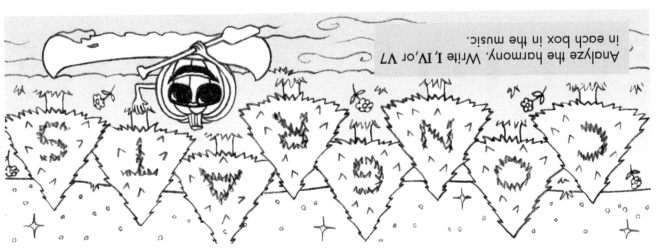

Analyze the harmony. Write I, IV, or V7 in each box in the music.

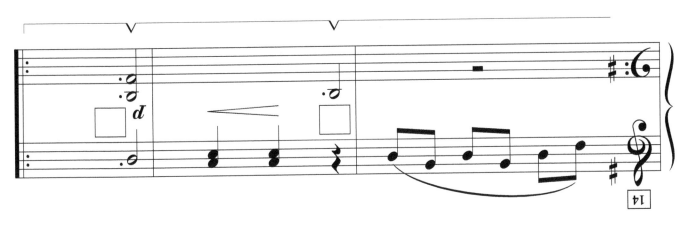

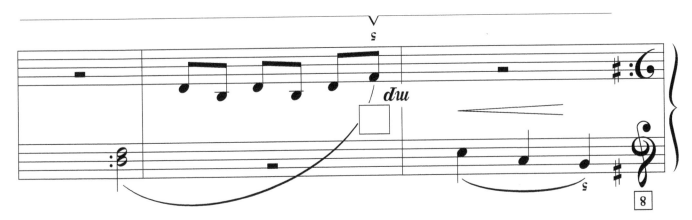

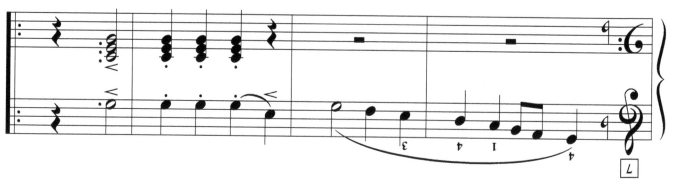

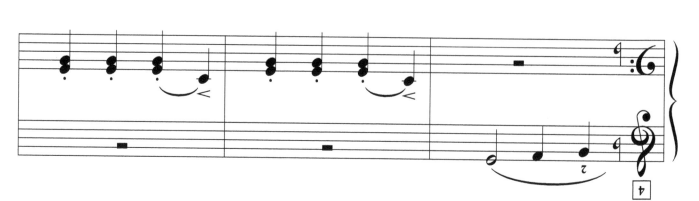

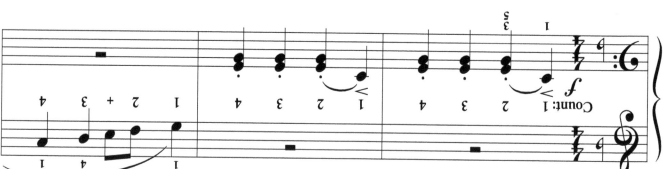

DAY 1: Turkish March

Key of _____ Major

Scan the music for R.H. B♭'s before playing.

DON'T PRACTICE THIS!

Draw the correct clef and **key signature** to form the F major scale.

Draw

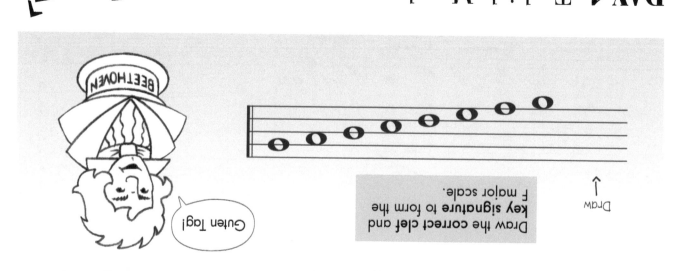

Guten Tag!

BEETHOVEN

DAY 2: Turkish March

Key of _____ Major

Scan the music for L.H. B♭'s before playing.

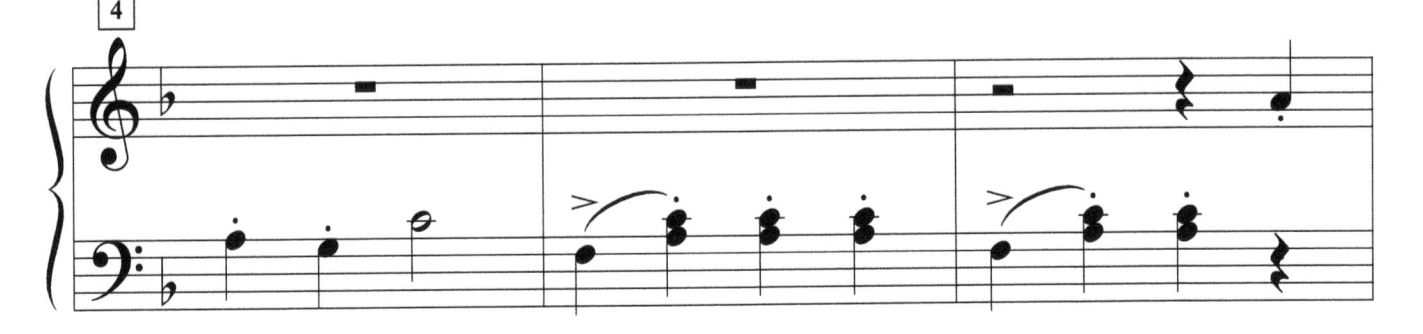

Spell my name by writing a **clef sign** and **whole note** for each letter. Can you write three different E's?

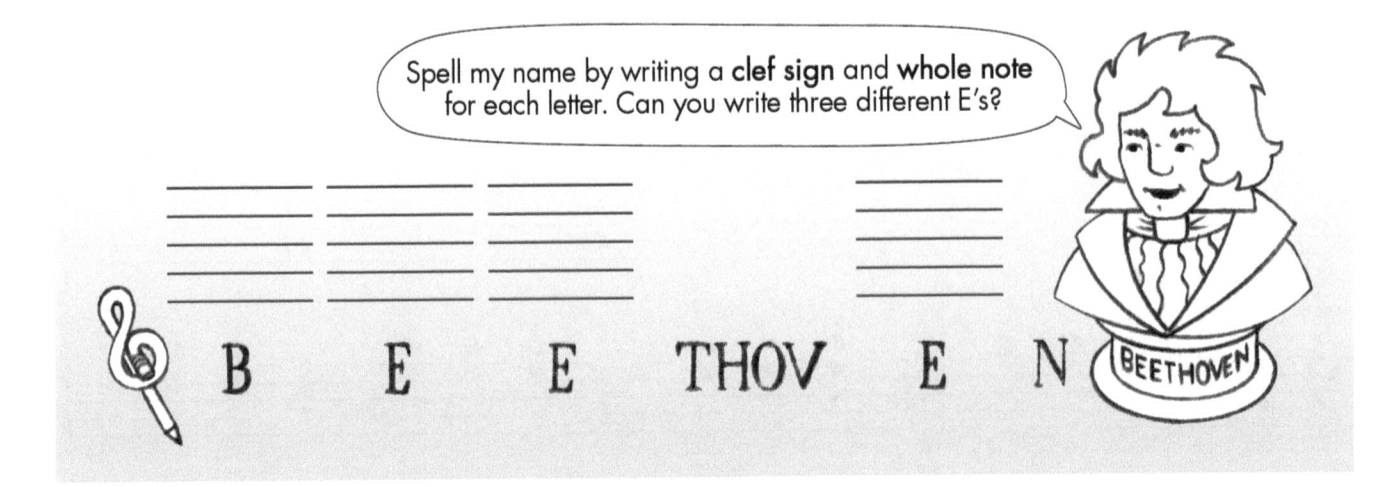

B E E THOV E N

BEETHOVEN

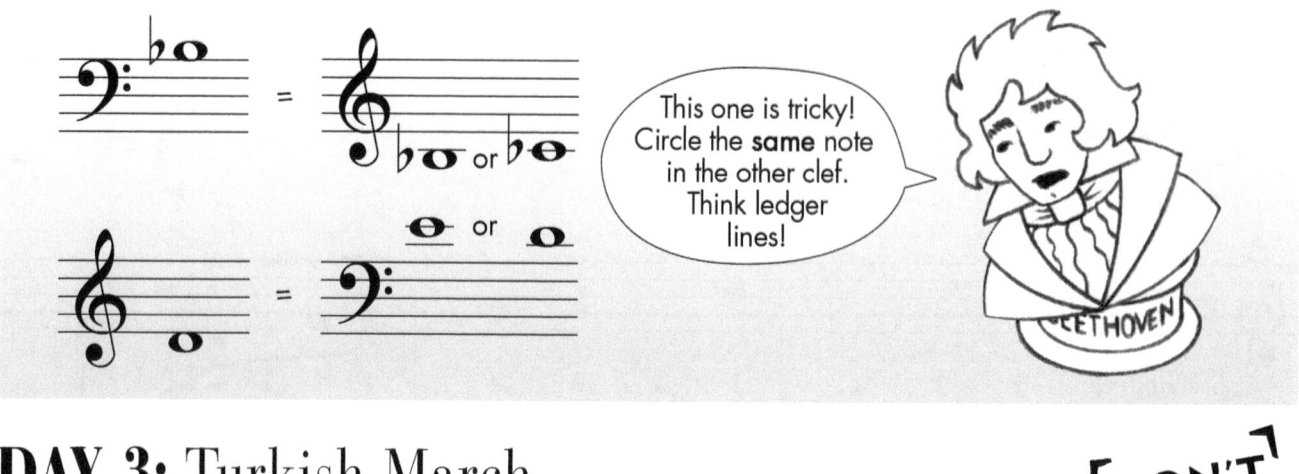

DAY 3: Turkish March

Key of _____ Major

Notice the L.H. starting position.

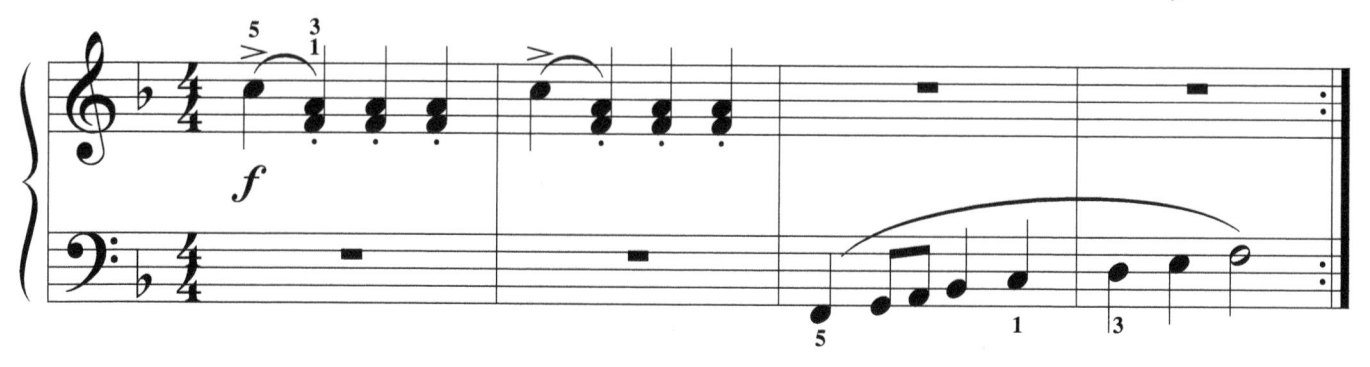

DAY 4: Turkish March

Key of _____ Major

DAY 5: Turkish March

Key of _____ Major

DON'T PRACTICE THIS!

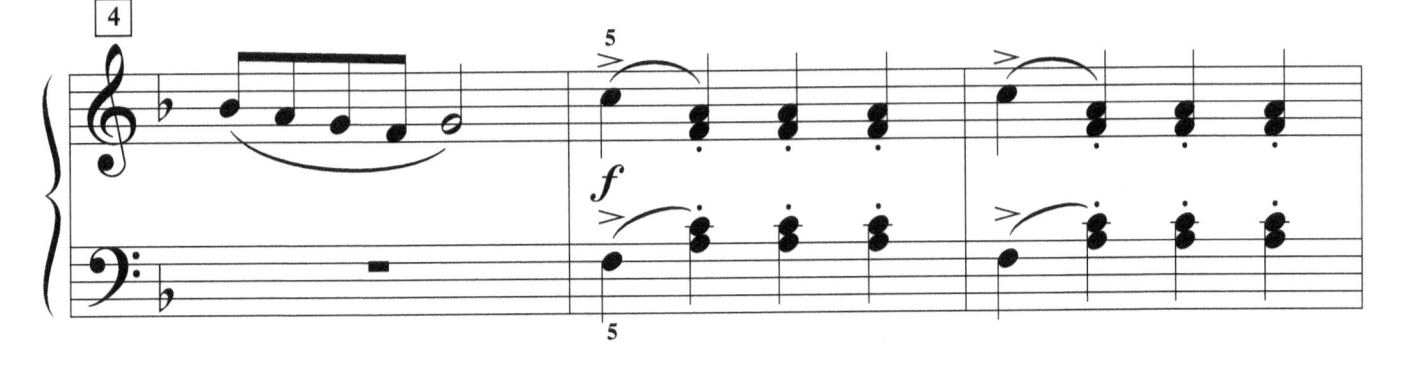

CONGRATS! Now write **two measures** of your own to complete this rhythm.

RHYTHM ROAD

(you write)   (you write)

BEETHOVEN

DAY 1: Auld Lang Syne

Key of _____ Major

Scan the music. Notice the ♩. ♪ rhythm pattern. Feel the dot on beat 2!

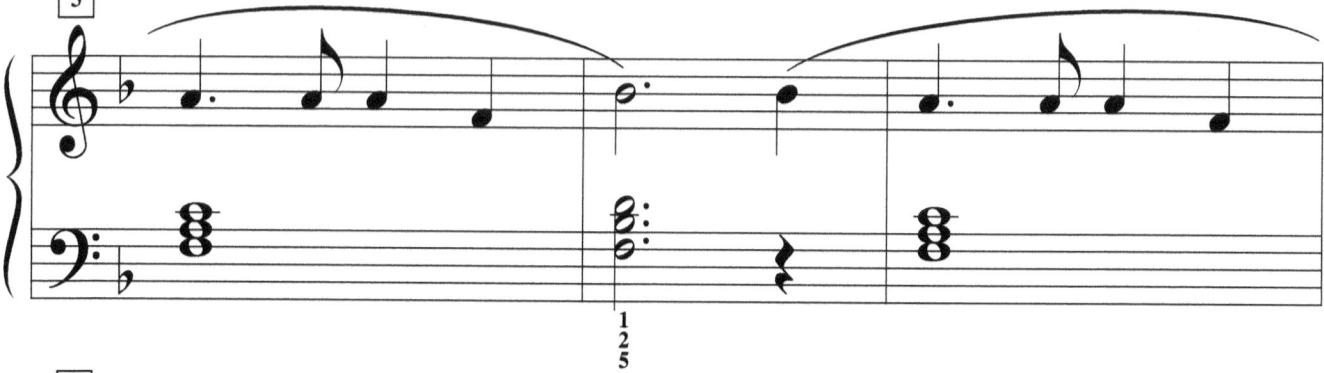

What chord is played with the highest note in the piece?
I, IV, or **V7** (circle one)

DAY 2: Auld Lang Syne

Key of _____ Major

DON'T PRACTICE THIS!

Scan the music. Do you see a rhythm pattern?

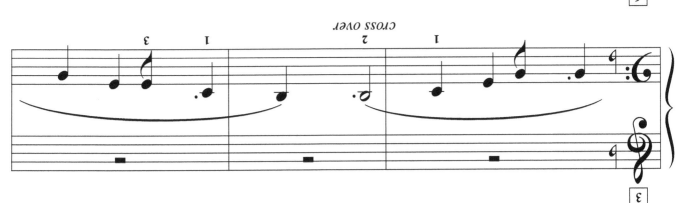

cross over

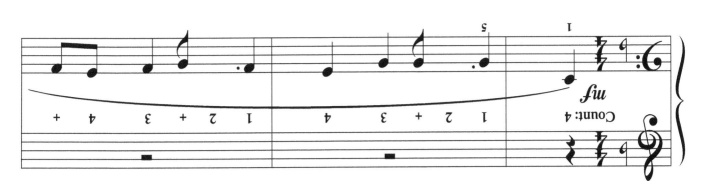

Count: 4

mf

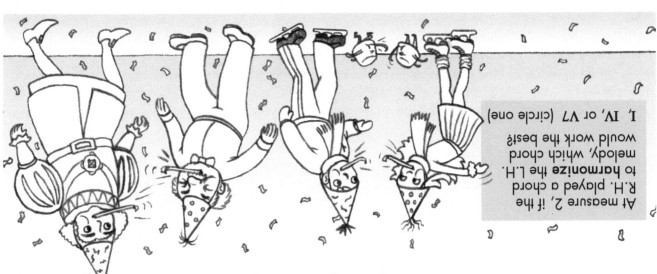

At measure 2, if the R.H. played a chord to harmonize the L.H. melody, which chord would work the best?

I, IV, or V7 (circle one)

Which line of music uses:
Only the **I** chord? Line ____
Only the **I** and **IV** chord? Line ____
Only the **V7** and **I** chord? Line ____

DAY 3: Auld Lang Syne

Key of ____ Major

DON'T
PRACTICE
THIS!

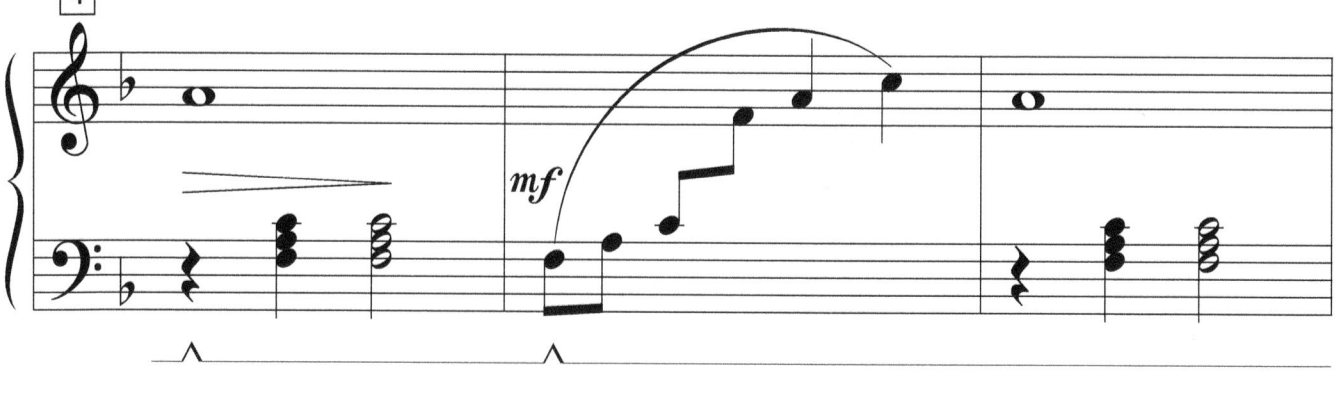

DAY 4: Auld Lang Syne

Key of _____ Major

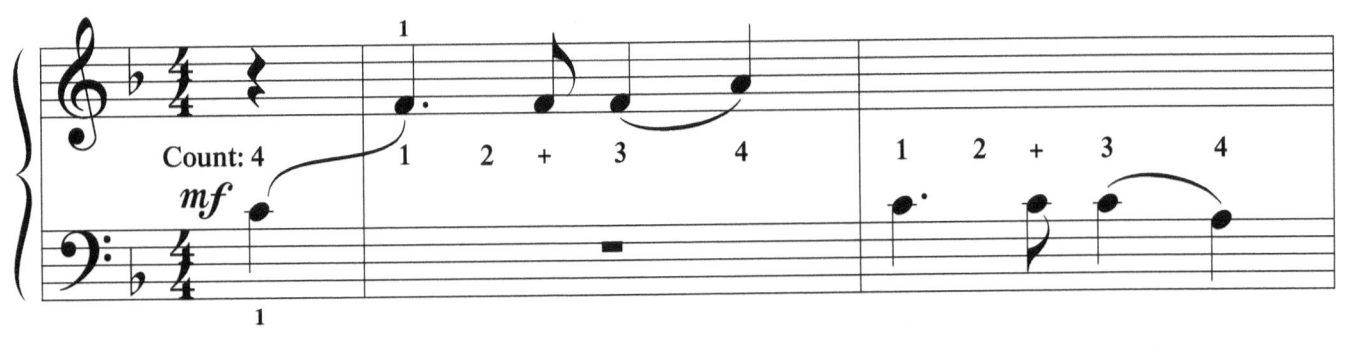

RHYTHM ROAD

Write the **one-measure** rhythm pattern used in this piece.

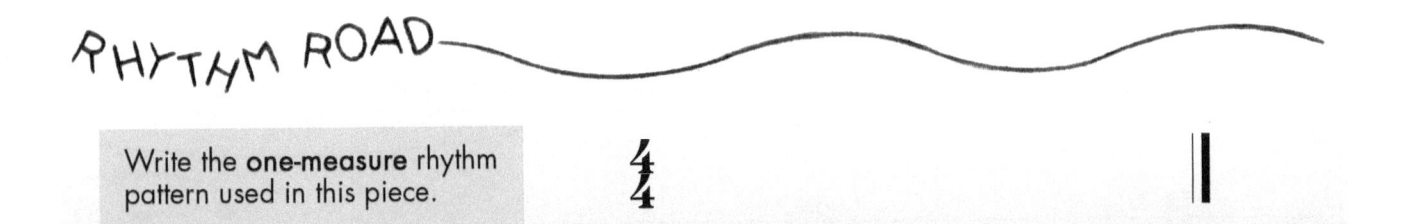

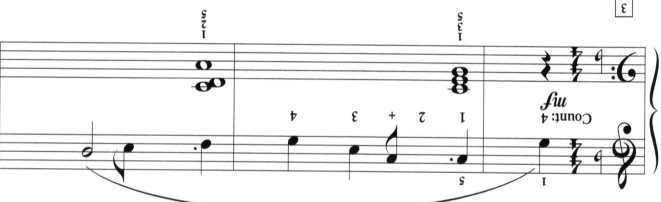

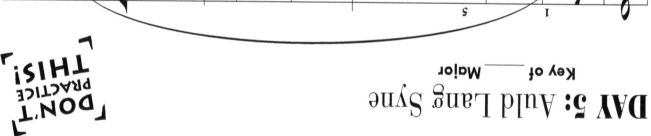

DAY 5: Auld Lang Syne

Key of _____ Major

DON'T PRACTICE THIS!

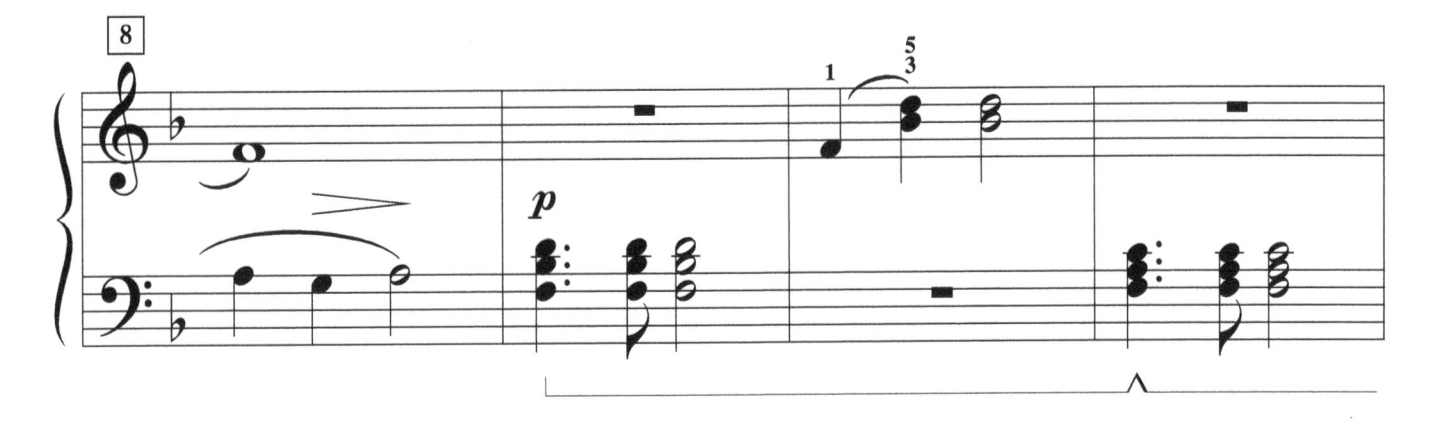

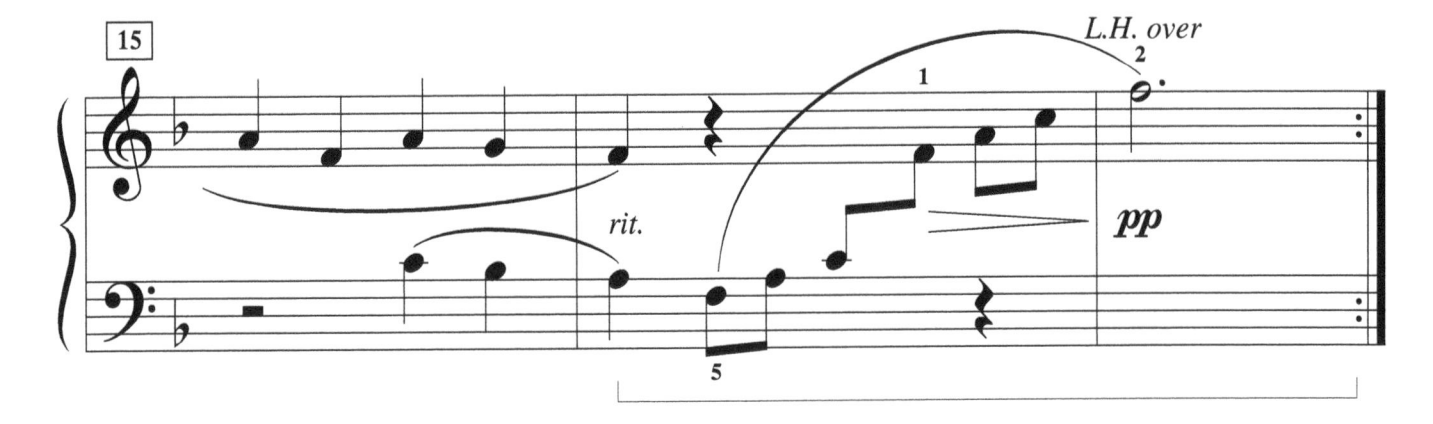

CONGRATULATIONS

Piano Adventures® Certificate

_____
(Your Name)

You are now a Level 2B Sightreader. Keep up the great work!

_____
Teacher

_____
Date